LEARNING
ENVIRONMENTS
BY DESIGN

Catherine Lombardozzi

PRESS

ATD Press is an internationally renowned source of insightful and practical information on
talent development, training, and professional development.

ATD Press
1640 King Street
Alexandria, VA 22314 USA

Ordering information: Books published by ATD Press can be purchased by visiting ATD's
website at www.td.org/books or by calling 800.628.2783 or 703.683.8100.

Library of Congress Control Number: 2015945442

ISBN-10: 1-56286-997-3
ISBN-13: 978-1-56286-997-7
e-ISBN: 978-1-60728-307-2

ATD Press Editorial Staff
Director: Kristine Luecker
Manager: Christian Green
Community of Practice Manager, Learning and Development: Amanda Smith
Developmental Editor: Kathryn Stafford
Associate Editor: Melissa Jones
Text Design: Maggie Hyde
Cover Design: Fatimah Weller and Tony Julien
Printed by Versa Press, Inc., East Peoria, IL

Contents

Introduction:
Designing Environments
for Learning

One of the most exciting aspects about working in learning and development is that the field is constantly changing. But that can also be deeply unsettling. Many years ago, I attended a learning industry conference that featured a number of thought leaders in panel discussions and keynote presentations. A recurring theme of their remarks was that "instructional design is dead." This was not something I wanted to hear—instructional design was the basis for a substantial portion of my livelihood. I taught instructional design in graduate courses. I managed a team of instructional designers. And I loved the part of my work that *was* instructional design—crafting graduate courses and professional workshops. I wanted to push off the comments as hyperbole, but they were being made by people whom I knew and respected in the field.

After the conference, I continued thinking about what these colleagues might know that I did not. What would make them pronounce instructional design dead? As I reflected, I came to realize that they were not really saying that there would be no more instructional design; that part of the message was indeed hyperbole (whether they wanted to admit it or not). There will always be a role for formal training and education programs. What they *were* saying was that instruction is only one of the ways we should consider addressing learning needs in our organization—they were predicting that other ways of supporting learning and development (L&D) would become more prominent.

With that insight, I decided to carefully consider all the other ways that people learn; it's a long list. As a learning strategist, I wanted to develop tools that would support me in considering a wider array of options, and I wanted to be able to explain the approaches to colleagues, clients, stakeholders, and students. From those ruminations came the notion of learning environment design. Over time, I developed a definition for learning environments, a wide-ranging list of potential components, and a process for designing a comprehensive approach to addressing learning needs that incorporates informal learning, social learning, developmental activities, and experiential learning, along with formal training and development activities. This book captures this framework and shares important additional lessons I have learned along the way regarding what makes learning environments work.

AN EMERGING ROLE FOR L&D

The toolkit for learning and development work has been expanding rapidly during the last several decades, along with the changing demands of learners. That expansion has been helped along by new technologies that make certain techniques possible and cost effective. Learning and development has a history of embracing a variety of new strategies and approaches to meet learners' ever-changing needs. If you look at the topics that have drawn attention at conferences and generated professional development programs over the years, you can see we are in a field that is not stagnant. We've seen the adoption of e-learning, collaboration on knowledge management systems, increasing capabilities for producing simulations, growing use of blended strategies, the incorporation of informal learning, and renewed attention to social learning, especially through social media.

Josh Bersin and Jane Hart, two prominent learning futurists, have both outlined trajectories showing how L&D has steadily incorporated e-learning, informal learning, and social learning approaches into what was once an industry primarily providing face-to-face training (see Figure I-1). They suggest that there will be a rising use of collaborative learning and integrated talent development moving forward (Bersin and Mallon 2009; Hart 2010). New technologies make a wider array of strategies possible (and cost effective) and new strategies have allowed us to be more responsive to changing learning needs.

One way that L&D leaders have responded to these changes is to make resources more accessible, which gives learners the opportunity to connect with others and share knowledge, both across the enterprise and with the wider world through Internet connectivity and social media. This expansion of strategies and services has not always been easy, and some L&D departments have not been able to fully embrace them due to reluctance, lack of resources, or opposition from client groups. Others have not adopted an array of strategies because they are not able to sort out how to do it effectively.

FIGURE I-1. THE EVOLUTION OF CORPORATE LEARNING

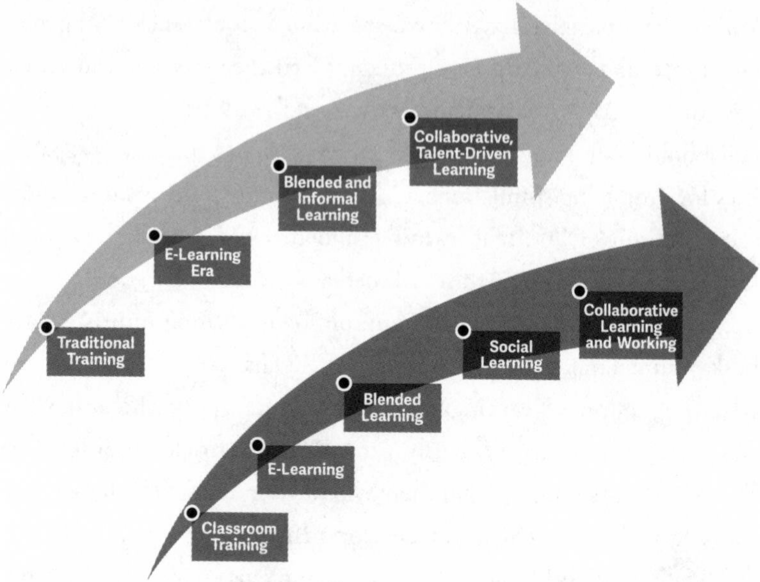

Top arrow adapted from Bersin and Mallon (2009); bottom arrow from Hart (2010).

Those who have embraced new technologies, meanwhile, have not always seen the anticipated benefits. A 2014 Corporate Executive Board (CEB) study concluded that while access to new resources and tools has increased, employees at all levels are struggling to be productive when taking advantage of them; people spend time learning, but are not getting enough useful knowledge and skill for their effort. One recommendation for correcting this problem is to guide learners to those resources, people, and activities that are most helpful.

Learning environment design offers a way of conceptualizing how to blend a variety of strategies into a coherent and valuable whole. A learning environment is a collection of resources and activities for learning, which is deliberately curated with a specific knowledge and skill development need in mind. Those resources and activities run the gamut, including reference materials and information resources (books, articles, videos, links); interpersonal connections with experts, coaches, and peers; formal learning activities such as training and degree programs; manager-led activities designed to support learning and development; and the learner's own on-the-job learning-by-doing activities.

The approach can be used by learning strategists, course designers, technology advocates, managers, and others to assemble a solid collection of resources to support learning for a specific skill set or knowledge base. Designing learning environments is a practical way to assist learners in managing their own development; it bridges the divide between structuring learning into courses and abandoning learners to the vagaries of an Internet search.

As the L&D department changes its focus from training to a more diversified portfolio of products and services, new roles will emerge for learning professionals. Among the most frequently cited is the role of curator, which we'll discuss at length in later chapters. There may also be more need for L&D practitioners to provide one-on-one assistance as advisers, coaches, and learning advocates. And the role of crafting learning strategy will likely require deep collaboration with technology experts and external providers in order to line up the most useful tools and resources for knowledge and skill building across the enterprise. This is the backdrop for the emergence of the learning environment design framework.

LEARNING ENVIRONMENTS IN CONTEXT

In today's workplace, we have two fairly distinct types of learning challenges. The first challenge is about communicating baseline knowledge and skill sets to people who likely don't know what they need to know. That's usually a curriculum challenge. The other challenge is helping people to deepen their knowledge and skill levels, and pick up additional learning as necessary in the course of engaging in a role. It can be daunting to consider how to support this kind of learning because multiple knowledge bases and skills are needed, each learner has varying levels of expertise, and one never really knows the optimal time to "teach" the next thing. This challenge is about supporting those with more individual, unique, and complex learning needs.

To explore these challenges, it might be helpful to imagine a few examples. For the first learning challenge, let's take a look at the needs of a young go-getter named Ralph. Ralph is a newly hired customer call representative who needs to learn about the company's products, systems, and workflows, along with the details of his roles and responsibilities, if he's going to get his career off on the right foot. He joins the company along with a cohort of soon-to-be peers, who will all be working in the same building and are all equally in the dark about the day-to-day details of their new jobs.

A scenario like this poses the kind of challenge that training was born to handle. Training is a great solution when learners have common learning needs, come in with similar backgrounds, and have the same kinds of tasks to fulfill. Training may be classroom based, e-learning, formal on-the-job training, or some combination thereof. Regardless of delivery method, the company can create a training program for Ralph and his peers that is well defined, well structured, and consistent for everyone. The company can also make additional courses and performance support materials available, to support and encourage growth after the initial new hire training.

For the other type of learning challenge, let's consider two other learners in the same organization, Cara and Yuri, who have been hired as salespeople. Their needs are driven individually, and the role they are asked to play in the organization requires an array of skill sets. Cara comes with a stellar sales record in another industry, while Yuri was hired from inside the organization based on his knowledge of the products and strong client relationship management skills. Both are highly motivated self-starters, and both have a strong desire to do well.

For Cara to be effective, she will need to learn about the company, products, and industry. Only then can she apply her exceptional sales skills to her new role. On the other hand, for Yuri to be effective, he will need to learn the sales process and strengthen his client influencing skills so that he can use his deep knowledge of the company and its products to effectively represent them in a sales situation. Both will work in the United States, but Yuri is based on the West Coast and Cara is in the New England office. They start their new jobs one month apart.

It will be more difficult for formal training to effectively address the kinds of needs that Cara and Yuri typify. There isn't enough commonality in background and need that would allow one formal solution to meet the learners where they are, and the hiring pattern is such that it would be difficult to get the minimum number of participants for a formal course, at least in a face-to-face or synchronous format. However, Cara and Yuri need to come up to speed quickly, so they need to learn just enough, just-in-time. No one program (even a boot-camp-style immersion) will work as a once-and-done solution for them.

This second kind of challenge is occurring more and more, as roles and skills become increasingly multifaceted and complex and learners come into a company anywhere along a wide continuum of knowledge base and skill level. Specific learning needs for these individuals—who may be dispersed geographically, sometimes even globally—come up at different times. The only things they may have in common are the topics on their learning plans: the knowledge base and skills needed to be effective. These learners need to be able to learn what they need when they need it—and they are capable of making the determination of what and when for themselves (or in collaboration with their managers). There may occasionally be instances when formal training makes sense for this group, but for the most part their learning needs should be addressed through other means.

Performance support and informal learning are sometimes touted as the best strategies for meeting these kinds of needs. The thinking goes that since these learners are self-starting individuals, it's possible for them to manage their own learning. Some people say that learning can be self-serviced with an Internet connection and the rich array of content it provides, such as articles, videos, education resources, social media, and communities of practice.

But that abundance of choice often creates decision paralysis. Too much energy is required to search for and vet resources, find the right people to talk to, and sort through all the noise to get to what is important. Rather than feeling unfettered and empowered, learners may feel lost and abandoned. There has to be a better way.

What can learning and development do for Cara and Yuri? L&D professionals can be immensely helpful if they can guide learners to the best resources; introduce them to thought leaders, potential collaborators, and peers; give guidance about the knowledge and skills needed to be successful; and embrace and teach practices that strengthen their abilities to learn both on the job and in hours between appointments. They can help create an environment in which learners can acquire the knowledge and skill they need in the time, place, and pace of their choosing.

A Learning Environment Strategy

A learning environment isn't necessarily a thing one can point to. It's a collection of resources and practices that enables the development of knowledge and skill. A learning environment is constituted by the people in a network, the books on their bookshelves, access to specific Internet materials, the support of their managers, and the ways learning happens every day just by working, as well as through other potential resources and activities. To learn at any given moment, people access whatever is available in their immediate vicinity, either physically close by or accessible through technology. In a very real sense, everyone lives in a learning environment. People are constantly engaged in activities and interactions that promote learning and growth, and surrounded by the people and resources that support it. There is a wide variety of tools for search and social interaction available.

A well-designed environment is conceptualized by designers or learning leaders in collaboration with subject matter experts and learners, and is deliberately curated to meet a specific learning need. This collection of components includes static resources, human connections, formal learning events, development strategies, and experiential learning practices.

An Example Environment for New Salespeople

What if the learning strategists and sales management team for Cara and Yuri worked together to identify and provide access to the most useful resources for their salespeople's anticipated learning needs? They might collect links to all the information Yuri needs to become an effective salesperson and all the resources Cara needs to learn the company's products and services. Other resources might include self-assessment tools, presentation templates, and job aids, as well as links to short e-learning modules and other brief formal courses that lay the groundwork for a specific knowledge base or skill. Introducing Cara and Yuri to people who can support them would also be important, so the company could provide a robust directory to help them easily find colleagues with specific knowledge and skills. The management team might also encourage them both to join a professional organization, which would provide additional resources and networking opportunities.

The sales management team could also ensure ongoing development by using monthly meetings as an opportunity to share success stories and debrief lost contracts, allowing the whole team to benefit from lessons learned. Managers may routinely "ride along" to observe salespeople in action—using the time to applaud and amplify what the salesperson is doing well and to provide developmental feedback. Salespeople might be actively encouraged to reach out to one another for advice and support, and a private microblogging tool could allow them to ping one another for quick answers and virtual high-fives for their successes. In some instances, forming mentoring relationships will also be helpful.

As highly motivated self-starters who are enthusiastic about the company and their role in its success, Cara and Yuri will also bring something to their own developmental efforts. They have both learned how to enhance their knowledge and skill through learning from their experiences, and they may share resources with one another and their other peers.

This combination of ingredients creates a fertile learning environment. The potential components are illustrated in Figure I-2, and additional information can be found in the learning environment blueprint in the appendix. The learning team could make all of these resources available through an easily accessible webpage on the company intranet. It's possible that these components could all come together without a lot of support from the L&D team, because Cara and Yuri are smart, self-sufficient people, and they will figure it out. However, when L&D plays a more strategic role in conceptualizing and promoting this kind of thoughtful aggregation of resources, it provides a highly valuable service.

FIGURE I-2: SALES TEAM ONBOARDING

Sales Team Onboarding		
Resources *reference materials and tools*	**People** *interpersonal connections*	**Training and Education** *formal learning activities*
Orientation • Home office in a box (how tos for systems and technology) • Transition playbook-information on clients in territory • Corporate onboarding resource site • Sales incentive information pages **Product and Industry Information** • Competitor intelligence materials (website links, analysis, white papers) • Sales portal (e.g., detailed product information, product briefing sheets, marketing materials, and archived sales team webinars) • Product apps for smartphones • RFP database (copies of all RFPs tagged with categories for easy search) • Sales bulletin and archive (e.g., a monthly newsletter including news, tips, profiles, and upcoming events) • Industry news feeds on intranet landing page **Sales Skills Resources** • Books provided electronically or in paper. • Success stories (e.g., an internally recorded series of interviews that break down lessons learned from big wins) • Trusted adviser webinar series (recorded) • Sales superstar podcast subscription (vendor materials about many topics available or downloadable) • Access to The Sales Professional article database • Suggested Twitter feeds	• Assigned mentor for onboarding period • Team profiles on company website (make it searchable and include skills profiles and client experience) • Sales team asynchronous discussion board and messaging tools • Quarterly regional informal get-togethers • Sales Institute membership (or similar professional organization)	• Sales simulation e-learning • E-learning series on company products • Consultative Selling course (publicly offered) • Corporate onboarding series • Annual sales conference (includes concurrent workshops on timely topics) • Monthly sales team webinars (topical education, usually about new products or competitor information)
	Development Practices *company-defined activities*	**Experiential Learning Practices** *on-the-job learning by doing*
	• Coaching guide provided to assigned mentor • Sales presentation coaching by the management team • Sales call partnering (ride-along) • Road Ready assessment (a sales manager checklist and assessment to validate whether new salespeople are up to speed) • All hands huddle conference calls (arranged by salespeople for assistance with time-sensitive challenges)	• Observations by experienced sales execs • Individualized coaching
Learner Motivation and Self-Direction		

Motivation and self-direction are both hiring criteria, and are thus assumed to be quite high for the salespeople's onboarding learning needs. Nonetheless, motivation and self-direction should be especially supported by videos of success stories, sales award programs, mentoring, or a monthly splash screen refresh (which could include a motivational message, usually about sales).

NOTE: All materials on component list are fabricated for illustration purposes.

ABOUT THIS BOOK

Learning Environments by Design shares a practical approach to designing a learning environment and provides background to help you ensure that what you build is effective for the learning concerns at hand.

Chapter 1 introduces the learning environment landscape, detailing its various components and strategies, and how they support learning and performance. Chapter 2 gives the nuts and bolts of learning environment design by describing a process flow and providing tools and tips for pulling a learning environment together and making it available for your learners.

Chapter 3 helps you look behind the scenes to understand more deeply what makes learning environments work by delving into what drives and ensures the effectiveness of self-directed learning. The most important supports for learning are usually human—the people who teach, coach, and demonstrate, for example—and chapter 4 summarizes some of what we know from research about how social learning works.

Chapter 5 explores how learning environment design can be applied to the creation of academic and student-support resources. The concepts described in this book can inform the design of open courses and MOOCs, as well as support professors who wish to have a broader and longer-term impact on their students and their field of study through creating learning environments for the topics and skills that are their areas of expertise. Academic administrators may also find learning environments useful for providing support services.

Chapter 6 examines where we're headed with regard to how learning is supported. Not only is training and development in a state of flux, but schools and universities are also rethinking their approaches. New technologies will no doubt continue to surprise, delight, and occasionally dismay us.

The appendix, "Learning Environment Blueprints," provides three case studies for further reflection.

THE BENEFITS OF LEARNING ENVIRONMENT DESIGN

Learning is ubiquitous and people in a wide variety of roles can benefit from understanding learning environment design.

Learning and development professionals in any role will discover new strategies and gain an understanding of the factors that enable learning. You'll be able to deliver more focused and impactful solutions to learning needs that are varied and emergent, and to position new tools and techniques with clients and colleagues.

Chief learning officers, learning leaders, and consultants will be able to envision how to align formal, informal, social, developmental, and experiential learning practices in a strategic way.

Managers who are concerned with supporting the development of the people on their teams will gain the ability to do that without relying on big budgets or constrained L&D resources. You'll see what you can do to recommend learning resources and support learning within your own group.

Faculty members and academic instructional designers can see how to break out of more traditional structures for learning, and add more open resources and social support for learning in an academic context.

Academic administrators will be able to conceptualize a way to bundle resources related to student services, such as student leadership development, academic support, and career services.

Learning technology leaders will strengthen their understanding of how various tools and techniques support learning, and will be able to better see how to link varied functionality into a coherent whole.

In addition to all the ways learning environment design can help you at work, these techniques can also provide guidance as you create your own environment for gaining the knowledge and skills you need. These ideas will help you to think through all the resources you could tap to support your own learning.

A LEARNING ENVIRONMENT FOR *LEARNING ENVIRONMENTS BY DESIGN*

A book can only take you so far in gaining the knowledge and skills that are helpful for creating learning environments. And it would seem a bit contradictory if the only avenue for learning about the subject was a single book. To that end, my website—www.L4LP.com—will link you to some additional learning environment design resources and activities, as well as to other people who are promoting similar ideas. You'll also get a listing of courses and seminars on the topic, conference presentations, and journal articles. Please be in touch with your stories and questions.

1

The Learning Environment Design Landscape

Learning theorists and researchers have come to understand that we don't so much "teach" as we create an environment in which people can learn. Learning facilitators design experiences and activities that allow people to grasp new concepts, learn required knowledge, and gain needed skills. More and more, these experiences and activities are embedded in the workplace rather than brought together in a formal course. Learning is a natural consequence of everyday interactions and ongoing work, and the need to gain knowledge and skills is more immediate and not able to be relegated to formal courseware.

When we need to support learning a specific knowledge base or skill, we need to expand the scope of our efforts into the workplace. We need to think about all the different ways that people learn and create an environment that makes learning resources accessible and gives people the support they need when and where they need it. That's the vision that learning environment design brings to fruition.

> *A learning environment is a deliberately curated collection of learning resources and activities related to a specific learning need.*

The environment metaphor is an important one—it's an image that encompasses all the components that surround living things. In a good environment, the components contribute to well-being and growth. In a well-designed landscape, for example, the environment includes sunlight, soil, water, and other elements, and the landscaper ensures the right elements to help the desired plants thrive. As defined here, a *learning environment* is intended to help people to learn and develop, and it, too, is designed using a wide range of components that support that endeavor.

LEARNING ENVIRONMENT COMPONENTS

To list all of the possible components of a learning environment would be as challenging as listing all of the possible plants to grow in a garden. Species of plants have multiple varieties, and new cultivars are created every day. In planting a garden, choices depend on climate, location, soil type, and gardener's preferences.

A similar process takes place when designing a learning environment. There is a world of options for resources and activities—and because new activities and resources are created regularly, it would be impossible to list all the possibilities. Even so, it's helpful to start with a solid list of potential components to include, such as those found in the learning components chart (Figure 1-1). This chart lists the six broad categories—resources, people, training and education, development practices, experiential learning practices, and learner motivation and self-direction—under which we can organize many different learning resources, activities, and practices.

Figure 1-1 enumerates a selection of the typical components that might be available in each category. These components can be curated into a learning environment to provide a wide range of possible supports for learning. Each project will have different particulars, and this list is not meant to be exhaustive; instead its aim is to prompt ideas for creating a robust, well-designed learning environment.

You'll notice as well that several of the categories suggest specific tools—such as blogging or microblogging tools, screen capture software, and video tools—not because the tools are learning assets, but because the learners can use them to create and add to the learning components available in the environment. Designers often include links to these kinds of tools when they create the learning portals that act as the entry point to the learning environment.

It's also important to notice how much of a learning environment is intangible, embedded in relationships and work practices. While an electronic portal is often useful for assembling materials and activities, the environment is physical and interpersonal as well as virtual.

FIGURE 1-1. LEARNING ENVIRONMENT COMPONENTS

Learning Environment Components	
Resources	• Performance support • Personal knowledge management • RSS feeds and other filtered information feeds • Shared documents and wiki spaces • Online databases and knowledge management systems • Books, articles, and Internet resources • Job aids • Podcasts and video-casts • Briefings (content delivery without activities) • Procedure manuals and technical manuals • Tools to support learner content sharing
People	• Peer support systems • Social media connections (blogs, microblogs, social bookmarking) • Group forums or discussion boards • Expert directories • Communities of practice • Mentor relationships and developmental networks • Coaching • Professional networks (live and online; professional organizations, user groups) • Conferences and professional meetings • Tools to support interaction
Training and Education	• Courseware and seminars (internal or external; in any delivery format) • Formal coaching after training • On-the-job training • Academic courses, degree programs, MOOCs (massive open online courses) • Certificate, certification, and licensing programs • Follow-up activities and exercises designed to support learning and application (enrichment and reflection activities) • Tools to support delivery of engaging learning activities
Development Practices	• Action learning programs • Stretch assignment management • Rotation and other experiential learning programs based in workplace activities • After-action review practices • Supervisor support, feedback, and coaching • Communication activities to influence learning readiness and application • Career coaching and development
Experiential Learning Practices	• Learning by doing • Engaging in critical reflection • Experimenting • Collaborating • Self-monitoring and analysis of outcomes and feedback • Creating personal notes, job aids • Teaching and creating resources for others
Learner Motivation and Self-Direction	• Desire to learn • Belief in link between learning and performance • Confidence in ability to learn • Self-directedness

Figure adapted from the author. Icons by Ayla Graney.

The list of components is compiled from a larger pool of potential items derived from industry models and long-term experience. Those familiar with the theories will notice elements of blended learning, transfer of learning, informal learning, and social learning theory and practice, along with ideas contributed by personal knowledge management and constructivist learning advocates. Looking across these streams of thought yields a very rich list of potential learning resources, activities, and practices, which were categorized to make identifying and selecting them a bit easier.

Resources

Under resources we can list all manner of materials that can be accessed to fuel learning. These may be physical resources like books, journals, equipment, or artifacts, or they may be electronically housed resources accessible using a computer and Internet. Databases, videos, electronic presentations, job aids, and manuals are also potential resources. When learners search the Internet for information or to find out how to do something, they are accessing resources. They might also go to a library or another physical space where reference materials and other learning assets can be found. Resources are useful for communicating explicit knowledge, which is valuable for people new to a role or task, as well as for supporting just-in-time learning and more direct performance support. The trick is finding resources that are at the right level, high quality, and relevant to a particular context. Learners need to take in the information and then figure out how to effectively apply it for themselves.

People

The people category recognizes the fact that relationships are critical to learning. Accessible face-to-face or online, people can offer wisdom, feedback, quick answers, insights, and modeling, among other things. In short, they provide the active interpersonal connections necessary for deep understanding and collaboration. These relationships can be deep (as with mentor and protégé relationships) or fairly distant (such as experts followed on Twitter). People communicate tacit knowledge through interpersonal interactions—teaching, mentoring, answering questions, and discussing—and they are co-learners and collaborators. While ubiquitous, learning through interactions with others is often far from a simple matter, requiring trust, effective communication, and follow-up. This is discussed in more detail in chapter 4.

Training and Education

Formal training and education are valuable when learner needs and course objectives are aligned. Training and education provide the framework around which to organize thinking and can be very useful for bringing people new to a role or task up to speed. Courses can be classroom-based, online, e-learning, self-study, on-the-job training, or offered in some combination of these modes. They may be for credit or not for credit; offered within an organization or by an educational institution, professional organization, or vendor. The degree to which people learn from training and education depends a great deal on the quality of the courses. Research has shown that retention and application depend on relevance, deep engagement, practice, and feedback.

The two component categories in the two bottom rows of Figure 1-1 highlight a range of learning and development practices. Learning is not just accomplished through drawing on knowledge and skills from other sources; it is often accomplished through processing one's own experiences.

Development Practices

The development practices category encompasses practices that the organization and its management team can implement to support learning. These practices require the active engagement of supervisors and managers, and play an important role in accelerating growth within the organization. Managers can ensure a culture in which self-directed learning can thrive through offering coaching and feedback as well as group reflection and continuous improvement activities. Development programs, on-the-job observation and feedback, strategies for sharing lessons learned among the team, and action learning projects are just some of the other ways that organizations support learning through development practices. In academic programs, there may be opportunities to regularly debrief work-based experiences and connect learners with one another on an ongoing basis. Specific development practices may also be listed under other categories (for example, mentoring could be a program under development practices or a relationship under people), but it's often important to identify the mechanisms for organizational and management support in order to ensure a culture that supports learning overall.

Experiential Learning Practices

The experiential learning practices category lists some of what individuals do (alone or with others) to make meaning of experiences and
transform them into concepts, ideas, and guidance for future action.
When you ask people to describe how they learn, one factor that
almost always comes up is learning by doing. Deep skill development
is facilitated through practice and reflection, and new knowledge is
created through action and collaboration. A designer or learning leader
doesn't necessarily create these experiences, but there may be ways to
promote specific kinds of experiences and to nurture learning from
them, most especially by making self-assessment and reflection tools
available to learners. Constructive feedback is often an essential part of
this learning process as well.

Learner Motivation and Self-Direction

Underpinning all these component categories is learner motivation
and self-direction. Learners need to choose to learn, so without some
degree of motivation, little learning can occur. (It's true that learning
can happen without conscious choice, but the kind of learning needs
we've been discussing in this book are more often those which learners need to recognize and choose to address.) Learner motivation is
the foundation for learning in all categories, and the components that
promote motivation and self-direction can be found in all categories as
well. You can imagine that some readings (resources) may be inspira-
tional, prompting people to want to learn more, or that some thought
leaders (people) may intrigue and exhort in ways that get potential

learners on board, so motivation is promoted through many different components (although not necessarily all). Self-direction is important because a learning environment strategy assumes that the learners will access materials as they need them. There is much more on this subject in chapter 3.

LEARNING ENVIRONMENT STRATEGIES

In the grand scheme, learning environments fit nicely among existing human resource development solutions, such as instructional solutions and performance-support solutions. Formal instruction is best when a specific set of learning objectives needs to be achieved, and instructional designers can employ solid instructional design processes and practices to address them. Performance support is called for when there is a need to provide immediate help in the workflow, and performance support specialists can suggest approaches that will enable that.

But when an assessment uncovers a knowledge or skill development need that can't be neatly addressed through instructional or performance support solutions, a deliberately curated learning environment may be the best way to provide the learning support required for people to engage productively in their own ongoing development.

There are many reasons why a learning leader might choose to design a learning environment; therefore, strategies are customized depending on the learning need and the characteristics of the learner groups they are meant to serve. The following sections discuss the four most likely scenarios.

Blended Learning Hub

As our electronic tools have grown, our blended learning strategies have gotten more sophisticated. Historically, blended learning has referred to some combination of e-learning, classroom-based learning, and coaching; however, more recently designers have found it valuable to cast a wider net for enrichment activities, application exercises, job aids, and support. Blended learning hubs are centered on the knowledge and skill targeted by a specific formal learning event, and the resources in this type of learning environment all rally around that event's topics. Often, these hubs are accessible only to those enrolled in the program, sometimes at the cohort level.

This kind of complex blended learning strategy is useful when you are trying to support the development of a complex skill, which learners will need to continue to practice and gain facility through real experience over time. It's important to support the on-the-job application of the skills with people, resources, and development practices that help learners continue to grow. The hub can also provide resources that help deepen learners' knowledge or skill as they become more agile with the core content and behaviors.

APPLICATIONS OF A BLENDED LEARNING HUB

Example 1: A university economics professor wants to support her students in the field, not only after specific courses, but also after graduation. She opens a personal website to provide quick access to Internet resources, seminars, and conferences that are likely to be of interest. The site also holds an annotated bibliography of recommended books. To keep things fresh, the professor actively posts to a Twitter feed that shares links to new articles of interest, and she also writes a blog where she discusses current events. Former students and other followers are invited to comment, and the professor engages in ongoing discussion around the topics of her posts.

Example 2: An organization wants to train its management team in the concepts and approaches of design thinking as a way of encouraging innovation. Learning strategists design a set of courses to teach core concepts, but they also support learning by making book recommendations, identifying a number of articles and websites that speak to these concepts, creating templates and tip sheets, offering coaching on crafting and facilitating meetings intended to use design thinking approaches, and publishing a blog that highlights design thinking stories from within the organization. They organize all these materials on a webpage available through the company's intranet.

Knowledge Exchange

The focus of a knowledge exchange is just that—giving interested parties the opportunity to share tactics, tools, results, and resources for the good of the practicing body as a whole.

This strategy works well when there is already a large body of accumulated knowledge that would be helpful for people new to a role or profession. It is also useful when knowledge and practices are quickly evolving, or when the learners are working on skills at an advanced level. A knowledge exchange supports advanced knowledge creation and allows experts to share their evolving knowledge so that less experienced people can access it.

EXAMPLE APPLICATIONS OF A KNOWLEDGE EXCHANGE

Example 1: A large consulting firm has associates deployed worldwide, and the knowledge they are accumulating through experience is also dispersed. A knowledge exchange provides an outlet through which consultants can share their experiences, documents, and lessons learned, so that others can search for material that might be leveraged for their own projects. For more immediate needs, the consultants can share their activities and expertise by using microblogging tools for short Q&A, posting their profiles (so that finding people with relevant knowledge and skills is easier), and writing blogs about their experiences. The knowledge exchange also aggregates recommendations for beneficial training programs and professional activities.

Example 2: A group of center city activists recognizes that they are learning what works and what doesn't through their own individual experiences, and they could increase their success by sharing what they know. They arrange to meet regularly to network and share their plans. In addition, they build an online space where they post resources, store documentation on their various campaigns, share a discussion board, and coordinate calendars so that everyone can learn from what others are doing (and occasionally find synergies).

Learning Resource Portal

In this scenario, the design focuses on creating a portal (Internet site) that aggregates a solid collection of formal and informal learning assets for an amorphous or diversified group of potential learners. The driving force here is featured content, rather than the assessed needs of potential learners.

This strategy is useful when the learners' needs diverge considerably, in such a way that it may be difficult to form a cohort with similar needs. A learning resource portal allows learners to self-select the materials and activities that best suit their development goals.

APPLICATIONS OF A LEARNING RESOURCE PORTAL

Example 1: A professional association of local architects wants to support its membership's learning needs. The members have many specializations and are at varying levels of expertise and tenure. A learning portal organizes a range of formal courses, certification options, videos, articles, books, blog feeds, discussion forums, and other learning materials for easy access. It even includes a listing of local architectural highlights with links to information about each building's architect and history.

Example 2: A workforce development team wants to increase the number of potential employees who have coding skills. They partner with a community college to offer an array of courses, and also create a website with links to other learning resources, many of which are free. The site includes information about potential job opportunities coming to the region and the necessary skills needed to apply.

Collaboratory

A collaboratory is among the most innovative of the learning environments because its focus is bringing like-minded people together so they can share and develop new knowledge and practices. Collaboratories feature tools and resources designed to support collaborative knowledge creation in addition to knowledge sharing.

This emergent learning environment strategy is particularly useful in cutting-edge areas of practice. Professionals in these environments are often using their own ingenuity to create what they need when they need it, and they are frequently experimenting with new practices. A collaboratory gives co-learners space to work together and discuss issues with one another, sharing their work, successes, and failures for the good of all.

APPLICATIONS OF A COLLABORATORY

Example 1: A talent development team in a large technology-oriented organization has decided to adopt a badging strategy to help track knowledge and skill sets across the organization, and to recognize ongoing development and accomplishments. (Badging is a way to recognize skill sets and contributions; "badges" are given to people by peers or governing bodies in recognition of an accomplishment or competence.) Colleagues working on the talent development strategy create an intranet space where they can share articles of interest in the emerging practice of competency badging, and where they can co-create and document the strategies they are crafting inside the orga-nization. A discussion board and instant messaging tool allows them to ping one another as new questions arise, so that they don't need to reinvent practices if others have already worked on similar projects. They often meet over coffee to discuss the organization's needs and to help one another brainstorm how to structure badging criteria.

Example 2: A local library converts its basement space to create a "maker lab" for inventors who want to take advantage of 3-D print-ing technology. It houses computers, a variety of 3-D printers, digital design software, and other equipment. A page on the library website contains links to a variety of relevant Internet resources. The lab offers workshops for entrepreneurs and hosts networking events. Most importantly, it is a place that encourages interaction among people with ideas.

Figure 1-2 summarizes these strategies. While the descriptions are helpful in considering the possible uses for learning environments, they are not all-inclusive or mutually exclusive. Often, learning environments incorporate elements of several strategies to meet a unique need.

CURATING AN EFFECTIVE ENVIRONMENT

When you curate the components for your learning environment, you do so primarily on the basis of the relevance and quality of the resources. A comprehensive learning environment contains components in each of the major categories: resources, people, training and education, development practices, and experiential learning practices (promoting motivation and self-direction can be accomplished within these components).

How do you determine whether you have enough of the right components to ensure you are giving your learners what they need? Your search begins with your purpose—as illustrated in Table 1-1, different purposes call for different types of components. Your learning environment may incorporate several purposes; you can determine which components work most effectively together by asking, "in order to achieve this purpose, what kind of components might learners want to access?"

FIGURE 1-2: LEARNING ENVIRONMENT STRATEGIES

Learning Environment Strategies		
Strategy	Purpose	Typical Projects
Blended Learning Hub	• Provide ongoing support for developing routine skills • Support application (performance)	• Management or leader development • Complex or deep skill building
Knowledge Exchange	• Support exchange of explicit knowledge • Capture and spread new knowledge • Provide database of information to quickly access as needed • Nurture a community of practice	• Product or process knowledge • Community of practice resources
Learning Resource Portal	• Improve learning efficiency; guide to most useful resources • Support building of deep knowledge base or skills • Improve craftsmanship	• Knowledge and skill building in existing fields of practice • Deepening competency over time
Collaboratory	• Share and develop knowledge • Rapidly advance practice • Provide support for solving problems • Support exchange of tacit knowledge	• Innovation initiatives • Rapid upskilling

The examples in the table are not meant to be all-inclusive; they simply demonstrate the process of thinking through what might be necessary to achieve a specific aim, and show how certain components more directly align with specific purposes. (The example purposes are drawn from Figure 1-2.)

TABLE 1-1. SUGGESTED COMPONENTS BY PURPOSE

Purpose	Suggested Components
Support exchange of explicit knowledge.	Knowledge databases, shared documents, procedure manuals, e-learning modules, job aids, training courses or education, after-action reviews, learning by doing
Provide ongoing support for developing routine skills.	Performance support, procedure manuals, role models, peer support, foundational training, e-learning demonstrations, practice exercises, structured feedback, coaching, learning by doing, experimenting
Support exchange of tacit knowledge.	Shared documents, peer support, social media, discussion forums, expert databases, after-action reviews, mentoring, collaborative projects
Improve craftsmanship; support building of deep skills.	Social media, communities of practice, professional networks, role models, mentoring, advanced education, coaching and feedback mechanisms, stretch assignments, self-assessment tools, collaboration and teamwork, learning by doing, critical reflection
Support application (performance).	Job aids, performance support resources, people to provide support and feedback, social media, discussion boards, supervisory support, tools for self-assessment and feedback, learning by doing
Capture and spread new knowledge.	Shared documents and wiki spaces, user-generated content sharing, social media, discussion boards, peer teaching, rotational assignments, after-action reviews, critical reflection, collaborative projects
Provide support for solving problems.	Shared documents, job aids, peer-support systems, expert directories, professional networks, on-the-job training, supervisory support, experimenting, collaborating
Nurture a community of practice.	Shared documents and wiki spaces, peer-support systems, social media, cohort or team training and education programs, action-learning programs, collaborating

LEARNING ENVIRONMENT DESIGN FRAMEWORK

Curating components and organizing them into a strategy for learning constitutes learning environment design, which exists within a larger system for learning and performance. The entire framework is captured in Figure 1-3.

The framework shows the overlap of performance and learning environments, and it highlights the components in each, which form a fairly complex system. Getting the lay of the land so that you can effectively conceptualize a learning environment therefore requires surveying a pretty big terrain, so let's take a look at each more closely.

The Performance Environment

We know from studies of human performance that performance outcomes are the result of interplay among a variety of factors, which include:

- Performer capability: The knowledge and skills an individual brings to a task.

- Expectations: The degree to which people know what is expected of them.

- Workflow and systems: The practices and systems (including computer systems and hardware) that enable the work to be done.

- Performance resources and tools: The support resources like job aids, manuals, and databases, as well as physical tools.

- Supervisory practices: How supervisors and managers enact their roles.

- Team dynamics: The quality of the interpersonal and work relationships among team members—how well they work together.

- Incentives and rewards: The structure and nature of formal and informal recognition for jobs well done.

These factors make up the performance environment, and the effectiveness of each of these systems and practices directly influences the performance outcomes achieved. Performance consultants know how to analyze the entire system to determine recommendations to improve performance or eliminate barriers. Describing all the factors related to human performance is beyond the scope of this book, but see the additional resources section for more comprehensive books on the subject.

Understanding the desired performance and related performance factors is an important prerequisite to creating environments that deliver valued outcomes. Before embarking on a project to support learning, it is important to understand the degree to which all other performance factors support the desired on-the-job behaviors. If there are any strong barriers or counterinfluences at work, then simply helping people gain knowledge and skills may not actually result in the desired performance and business outcomes; energies may be better spent elsewhere. When learning projects fail to affect performance, that failure can sometimes be traced to the fact that employee capability was not the only—or most important—factor that needed to be changed in the performance system. (For example, work procedures weren't supportive, or supervisory practices needed work.)

If your front-end needs assessment shows that increases in knowledge or skill (performer capability) will positively affect performance, then you've got a bona fide learning need. (See chapter 2 for more on assessment.) There are many strategies to support learning, and designing a learning environment is one way to align a number of those strategies to a common goal.

FIGURE 1-3. LEARNING ENVIRONMENT DESIGN FRAMEWORK

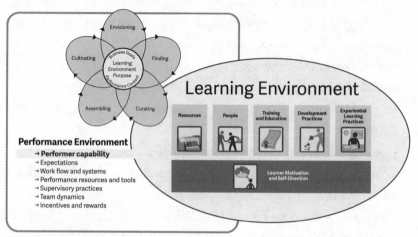

Figure adapted from the author. Icons by Ayla Graney.

The Learning Environment

As discussed, the learning environment is made up of resources, people, training and education, development practices, experiential learning practices, and learner motivation and self-direction. The fact that components in the learning environment are also part of the performance environment is an interesting dynamic. The learning and performance environments overlap; some learning is embedded in the performance environment (for example, collaborating on a project, accessing performance support tools for learning), and some learning is accomplished by stepping outside the performance environment (mentally or physically) for a brief period. Assets that support performance can sometimes also be leveraged for learning, and vice-versa.

The Learning Environment Design Processes

The learning environment design processes of envisioning, finding, curating, assembling, and cultivating are applied to designing the environment as a whole. These processes are discussed in detail in chapter 2. To some degree, these processes can also be applied to designing a performance environment.

As you can see, learning environment design exists within a very dynamic context. Achieving desired performance can be a complex task, as can ensuring that people have the requisite capability to do their part. Too often, formal learning events alone don't account for this complexity, and they only attempt to affect a small portion of the whole system. That may well be appropriate for some needs, but with a well-curated learning environment in play, you have a much better opportunity to support people in developing the knowledge and skills they need to succeed.

RELATED IDEAS

There are a number of related ideas that can be leveraged to conceptualize a designed learning environment. You'll find more information on these ideas in the additional resources section and on my website (www.L4LP.com) if you want to explore them further.

Learning Ecosystems

Definitions vary, but in general a learning ecosystem is the combination of people, processes, technologies, and content that support learning and performance. In their 2014 whitepaper, Marc Rosenberg and Steve Foreman defined a learning and performance ecosystem as one that "enhances individual and organizational effectiveness by connecting people and supporting them with a broad range of content, processes, and technologies to drive performance." The components in their model include performance support, knowledge management, access to experts, social networking and collaboration, structured learning, and talent management. Like any ecosystem, a learning and performance ecosystem is constituted by its interdependencies; the parts don't work nearly as well if they are out of sync with one another. The "ecosystem" label is appealing because it conjures a metaphor about growth, cyclical regeneration, and mutual support that feels appropriate when we are discussing how people learn in dynamic organizations. While the terminology is still evolving, learning ecosystems seem to be under discussion when learning leaders are trying to strategize the organization's culture and infrastructure as it relates to supporting learning. A learning ecosystem is writ large. On the other hand, a learning environment, as discussed in these pages, is related to a specific learning need and learner group. Learning environment designers select the relevant aspects of the learning and performance ecosystem to curate a set of resources and activities for learning a specific knowledge base or skill in context. The ideas behind the terms *ecosystem* and *environment* go hand-in-hand, and many people will interchange them.

Personal Learning Environments

Also called personal learning networks or personal knowledge management, a personal learning environment (PLE) encompasses a collection of resources, people, and practices that an *individual* pulls together to support his or her own learning. PLEs often have many technological components, because the Internet opens pathways to abundant resources, and we have access to electronic tools (storage, presentation tools) that have proven quite useful for supporting and promoting self-directed learning.

Communities of Practice

A community of practice is based in the interactions among a group of people who have a common domain of practice; who share similar processes, procedures, tools, and approaches (often with a specialized language as well); and who genuinely want to advance their knowledge and practices by interacting with and supporting one another. In this context, the community is primarily defined by the people and their interpersonal relationships, but these days there is often a website, discussion board, or communication tool offered as well to support openness among community members.

Environments Conducive to Learning

It's interesting to note that teachers and facilitators often talk about creating "an environment conducive to learning" (also called a learning environment) by which they mean creating a space in a classroom, home, or workplace that acts as a petri dish for learning and growth. Generally, they are talking about characteristics that are not tangible, such as openness, tolerance for experimentation or potential failure, and psychological safety. A positive environment for learning could also be a place where certain encouraging behaviors (such as helpful feedback, genuine caring among people, collaboration, or coaching) are common. Even the features of the physical environment can contribute to learning: the quality of the light and sound, the comfort of the furnishings, and the potential of being surrounded by others who are also learning. A successful learning environment (as defined here) represents many of these characteristics as well.

CONCLUDING THOUGHTS

The core idea in learning environment design is to provide learners with more support in finding and accessing learning resources when and where they need them. Savvy learners have always been able to manage on their own, and they have been given a real boon with the explosion of available materials and connections on the web. But that massive amount of material also has drawbacks—it takes time and judgment to find the right materials, and many learners don't have the time or background to adequately judge the quality and applicability of the resources they find. They may not know about the leading thinkers and experienced experts in their companies or their fields. They may not even be able to describe the competencies they need to become more effective in their roles.

Learning professionals can draw together specific materials and activities that they have vetted to support learners in developing their knowledge bases and skills. The concepts and processes laid out in this book may help you imagine how this might be achieved. With the high-level framework in mind, we can now explore the approach and theories behind it in more detail.

2

The Learning Environment Design Processes

Learning environment design can be likened to landscaping. Beautiful gardens do not typically spring up fully formed, but instead are carefully planned and cultivated. The flowers themselves are naturally occurring somewhere, but the creation of a flourishing landscape in a particular place that suits the desires of the landowner often takes the talents of landscape architects and gardeners who select the best plants, design a pleasing arrangement, and create a supportive environment in which they can grow.

The same can be said of learning. Human beings learn all the time; it's a natural process in many ways. But if we want learning to be cultivated, if we want to influence what is being learned, and if we want to nurture learning, then we need to shape the environment in which it occurs. Learning professionals create environments in which learning flourishes.

The learning environment design framework provides would-be learning gardeners with the tools to create rich environments for learning. Just like a gardener follows a process to cultivate a picture-perfect patch of earth, an L&D professional uses a flexible learning environment design process to support deep learning. Some gardening projects are not all that complicated, simply calling for quick purchase and planting. Others are botanical gardens with a large array of plantings and many hands to do the work; these become a transporting experience for those who enter. Learning projects are like that, too. While the same general processes apply, some are down-and-dirty, whereas others are rich and robust.

Learning environment design has five major processes that work together to create and continuously enrich an environment. Developing a learning environment is a lot like improving the landscaping around your home, in that it builds on what is already there. In assembling a learning environment, you are highlighting and shaping the available elements, while adding and juxtaposing additional elements that enrich the space and make it more useful.

At the center of your planning and thinking are the business goals and performance context from which the learning needs arise. It is critical that you first understand what the organization is trying to achieve, and how knowledge and skill will be put to use in day-to-day work. That context drives your purpose, and purpose centers your design efforts.

The processes for designing an environment are organic and iterative. The broad learning and performance ecosystem provides plenty of material to incorporate into a deliberately curated environment.

The landscaping terminology used in this book and the daisy-shaped design graphic (Figure 2-1) capture the active dynamics of the overall learning environment design processes.

FIGURE 2-1. LEARNING ENVIRONMENT DESIGN PROCESSES

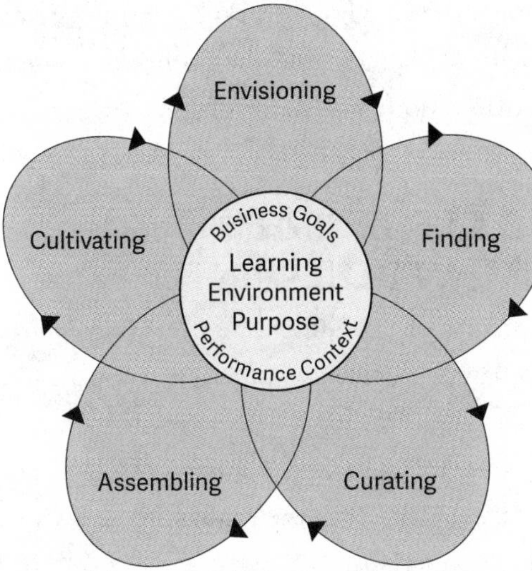

Designing a learning environment involves five overlapping processes, which we will discuss in depth in this chapter:

- **Envisioning:** Imagining the purpose, context, and components of the learning environment.

- **Finding:** Locating a range of resources and activities that are on topic.

- **Curating:** Using expert judgment to recommend the most relevant and useful components for the learning environment's specific learners and purpose.

- **Assembling:** Collating and packaging the resources and activities, and making them available to your learners.
- **Cultivating:** Ensuring that the environment continues to be fresh, enticing, and useful.

Unlike the design of a learning event, a learning environment is never really complete; it is constantly evolving. You assemble a curated set of components for launch, and then continue to grow and shape them as the organization's goals and the learners' needs change and expand over time.

DRAFTING A LEARNING ENVIRONMENT BLUEPRINT

While in the process of designing a new learning environment, it is often useful to have a blueprint—a one- or two-page document that illustrates the overall vision for the package of resources you plan to collate. The document helps you to communicate your vision to learners and other stakeholders along the way, and it is easy to revise as you get feedback and suggestions.

In general, a learning environment blueprint contains the following information:

- Identification of the **business goals and performance context** that are shaping the need for a learning environment (determined in the envisioning process).

- A description of the **purpose** of the environment—what it is that you are trying to achieve (determined in the envisioning process).

- A description of the **learners** the environment is intended to support, including characteristics relevant to creating an environment for them—such as the number of learners, geographic dispersion, and access to and familiarity with computers and Internet (uncovered in the envisioning process).

- A description of the **topic and scope** of the environment—the knowledge or skill being learned and the intended depth of the resources (determined in the envisioning process).

- A list of learning **components** (put together in the finding and curating processes), organized in ways that make sense to the stakeholders.

- A **sketch or prototype** of the portal or package that will be used to make the environment available to the learners (a product of the assembling process).

- A **plan** for evolving and cultivating the environment—including strategies for learner-generated content and ongoing evaluation and maintenance (a starting place for the cultivating process).

When documenting a blueprint, take into consideration the needs of sponsors and stakeholders, crafting a short document that paints a picture that will inspire their imagination and address any concerns you anticipate. The elements of the blueprint should build on each other and serve as a framework for communication. The first four parts—business goals and performance context, purpose, learner description, and topic and scope—succinctly summarize the project so you can recruit people for finding and curating. Adding a list of components and conceptualizing how they need to be organized gives a solid vision to those who you may need to help you assemble or prototype the environment. Adding the sketch or prototype to your documentation puts you in a position to garner support for the additional resources that may be necessary to bring the environment to fruition. To cap off your blueprint, you may want to provide your stakeholders with a plan for ongoing care for the environment, such as recommendations for ownership, community managers, or site maintenance if applicable.

A complete blueprint is usually the product of an initial first run of all the design processes. Your needs assessment leads to envisioning, where you set the overall direction for what you want to achieve; finding and curating will give you a start list of components that you'd like to pull together. Finally, thinking through the assembling and cultivating processes will allow you to sketch your vision and assess the ongoing needs related to keeping the environment fresh. *Keep in mind, though, that your blueprint has to remain flexible throughout the process; additional work on the project often leads to adjustments in details that were previously penciled in.* See the appendix for three example blueprints.

ENVISIONING

Envisioning is imagining the purpose, context, and components of the learning environment. It is both a design step and an emergent process after the initial environment is launched.

Envisioning encapsulates these activities:
- determining the need for a learning environment
- defining the learning environment purpose and context
- getting to know the learners
- solidifying the topic and scope
- crafting a blueprint.

In one sense, envisioning is creating a complete blueprint for your environment so that you can share it with stakeholders for feedback and appropriate approvals. But at its core, envisioning is the process of defining a purpose for your learning environment; identifying the learners, topic, context, and limiting parameters that will help to shape and scope the environment you create. The core aspects of envisioning set the stage for all the other processes, which then feed the overall vision as the environment comes together.

Before envisioning—indeed, before even deciding that a learning environment is an appropriate strategy for your project—you will need to do some level of needs assessment. Using your toolkit of assessment techniques, you need to learn as much as you can about the project, the learners, and the learner's needs. (A full discussion of needs assessment techniques is the subject of other books; a few of my favorite resources are referenced in the additional resources section.) If it's not already part of your up-front assessment process, be sure to gather information about the business and performance goals related to the project. And, in addition to learner demographics and the information you gather to help define needs, you should explore how learners and related experts interact with one another and other facets of the learning culture.

Determining the Need for a Learning Environment

If your needs assessment shows that knowledge and skill development is necessary, you have a huge array of possible responses to address that need. Traditionally, learning professionals have selected one type of response: formal learning, in the form of a course, an e-learning module, or other structured component. But increasingly we have the kinds of complex learning needs that can't be addressed by one solution. That's when a learning environment makes the most sense. You need to use your judgment to determine whether the learners will benefit from having learning resources and activities compiled for their use.

How do you know when a curated learning environment would be a valuable way to support learners in developing their capabilities? There are a number of characteristics of learners, their environment, and the nature of the content that point to the need for a learning environment. Indicative characteristics include:

- The learning topic is a complex skill, requiring a deep knowledge base.
- The knowledge and skill is likely best developed over time through on-the-job experience and practice, even if some baseline training is also warranted.
- The knowledge and skill to be learned is more tacit than explicit.
- The knowledge and skill sets are constantly emerging.
- The learners' needs with regard to the knowledge base or skill set are diverse, or the context in which they apply them varies.
- The learners are self-motivated and capable of managing their own learning.
- The learning culture supports experimentation and peer-to-peer learning.

In addition to asking questions that assess these factors, you might consider asking broad questions up front that can help you determine the degree to which a learning environment already exists for the learners. You could ask some of the following questions to gain information about each of the learning environment component areas:

- **Learner Motivation and Self-Direction**
  - o What are learners motivated to learn?
  - o How is their identity and success tied to ongoing learning?
  - o What hesitation or resistance to learning (if any) seems to exist?
  - o What is the cause of that hesitation?
  - o To what degree do learners manage their own learning?

- **Resources**
  - o What information and resources do performers use to support the learning needed to make them competent for performance?
  - o What is the technical environment for learners (degree of access to computers and the Internet)?

- **People**
  - o How are learners connected to one another and to experts in their field?
  - o What are the characteristics of the interpersonal environment and team environment for learners?
  - o What tools or processes are available to connect learners to other people who can support their leaning?

- **Training and Education**
  - o How do learners learn the foundation for their roles?
  - o What courses and programs exist to put learners on the right track?

- **Development Practices**
  - o What supervisory practices and company programs are in play that support or inhibit learning?
- **Experiential Learning Practices**
  - o What is the environment for learning by doing?
  - o To what degree are mistakes or failure tolerated?
  - o What practices promote reflection?

Defining Learning Environment Purpose and Context

A clear vision for a learning environment articulates what you want the environment to do to support learning and performance—its driving purpose and context.

Instructional designers are generally urged to write clear and measurable learning objectives for their projects, and to link them to on-the-job performance objectives and business goals. A learning environment, however, works differently from instruction. A learning environment plays a supporting role in helping learners meet *self-defined* learning objectives. To try to list all of those potential learning objectives as a foundation for learning environment design would be an impossible task.

Learning environment designers don't specify what learners will know, value, or be able to do as a result of their encounter with the learning environment; the learners do that for themselves. Instead, they assemble a learning environment in anticipation of the emerging learning needs their targeted learners may have related to the given topic.

A few examples might clarify the distinction between instructional goals and learning environment goals, especially for those well-schooled in writing learning objectives for their projects.

Let's say, for example, that you are designing a learning environment for salespeople, and part of your purpose is to help them to learn about competitor products. Consider how they might use that knowledge: Maybe they need to be able to write a detailed comparison chart for a client with particular priorities. Or, maybe they need to anticipate how products compare in general. If you were going to define learning objectives for training, you would realize that each application requires a different angle and level of detail. With a learning environment solution, you might conceptualize your purpose as connecting your learners to information—in this case, specific areas of competitor websites and industry review articles. You let the learners sort out what they need to learn in order to do their jobs effectively.

What if your project is to support woodworkers in improving their craft? The list of potential knowledge and skills that learners may want to develop is enormous. Some of those needs may be met by formal training in your environment, but the scope of learning support needed is much broader. Your purpose in designing a learning environment is to scaffold the ongoing development of skills and provide support for solving problems.

Or, your project may be to facilitate learning among people who are working in a leading-edge technical area. Learning objectives don't make sense here because the learners have to learn through active experimentation and rapid iteration. The purpose of your learning environment might be to rapidly advance practice or to build a community of practice, both of which require a more active, learner-driven collection of resources, tools, and activities.

Remember that learning environments are a solution meant to enable self-directed learning, so the learners define their own goals. The learning environment purpose statement clarifies how you mean to support them in achieving their goals and guides your design decisions. Table 2-1 compares the goal-setting approaches used for instructional design and learning environment design.

TABLE 2-1: COMPARING INTEGRATED OBJECTIVES FOR INSTRUCTIONAL DESIGN AND DRIVING GOALS FOR LEARNING ENVIRONMENTS

Integrated Objectives for Instructional Design	Driving Goals for Learning Environments
Business Objectives The business goal or initiative that your project supports.	**Business Goal** The business goal or initiative that your project supports.
Performance Objectives The observable on-the-job behaviors that the program is intended to impact.	**Performance Context** The on-the-job behaviors that are to be developed or affected by the learning environment.
Learning Objectives What learners will know, value, and be able to do at the conclusion of the training program.	**Purpose** What the learning environment is intended to achieve, related to its topic and scope.

Based on Hodges (2001).

The **purpose** is what the learning environment is intended to achieve, related to its topic and scope. Your purpose is driven by the performance context and business goals. Remember that in the design processes diagram (Figure 2-1), all three of these facets were depicted as the core around which the learning environment design processes revolve.

Typically, you identify the business goals and performance context before making the recommendation to design a learning environment, although these may need to be fine-tuned later on. Your environment's purpose comes out of a thorough understanding of the overall context and learning needs.

The **performance context** defines on-the-job behaviors that are to be developed or affected by your learning environment. In some instances, you may be able to determine specific performance objectives that document what the learners should be able to do on the job (similar to instructional design), but that is not always the case because learners may be in different roles. The performance context provides an anchor and a top-level filter for finding and curating resources for the learning environment. Without a performance anchor, you might be tempted to include a lot of topical materials that would not be relevant or useful to learners.

There's another reason that understanding performance context is an important up-front consideration. As part of your exploration of the performance context, you seek to ascertain the degree to which learning can affect performance. Often, when there is a performance issue of some kind, knowledge and skill gaps are not actually the most significant barriers to performance. If people are going to invest their time in deepening their knowledge or updating their skills, you need to be sure that those improvements are likely to result in solid, on-the-job performance. It's possible that other performance interventions might have more impact, such as removing system constraints, aligning goals and incentives, or providing thorough feedback. A learning and development plan will only affect knowledge base and skill, and if these are not the most important contributors to performance or the reason for performance gaps, then devote your time and energies elsewhere. A full discussion of this kind of performance consulting is outside the scope of this book, but a short list of recommended resources on this topic is included in the additional resources section.

Another important contextualizing factor is understanding the **business goals** that require the capabilities your learning environment supports. Business goals justify the energy required to design and cultivate a learning environment by generating the performance objectives and the human capability required for that performance (some of which may need to be learned). It may be more difficult to identify the specific business goals being supported if your learner group comes from differing companies, departments, or contexts. But it is worth the effort to explore or hypothesize the kinds of business goals that might be affected in order to create a relevant learning environment.

With the business goals and performance context in mind, you should be able to define your learning environment's purpose. The purpose statement usually begins with an action verb—what you want the environment to do for the learners. You'll be able to evaluate the achievement of that purpose by surveying the learners or looking for a change in learner capability or learner performance outcomes.

You should articulate the purpose of your learning environment specifically for your situation, but we discussed a number of possible purpose statements earlier (see Table 1-1), which you may be able to leverage. Here are some of those examples:

- Support exchange of explicit knowledge.
- Provide ongoing support for developing routine skills.
- Support the exchange of tacit knowledge.
- Improve craftsmanship; support building of deep skills.
- Support application (performance).
- Capture and spread new knowledge.
- Provide support for solving problems.
- Nurture a community of practice.

Write a clear purpose statement in your own words, stating what you and the learners want to achieve with this environment. It isn't necessarily important to determine which strategy— blended learning hub, knowledge exchange, learning resource portal, or collaboratory— matches your particular project because they often overlap. However, keeping a particular strategy in mind can provide helpful shorthand for what you are trying to achieve.

Getting to Know the Learners

The learner group is usually defined by job role or by identifying people who do a specific kind of task. You identified the learner group when you defined the project, but it's useful to deepen your understanding of the people who will access the environment as you start to envision the details. To aid your decisions about curating and assembling it is helpful to know how many learners you have, their geographic dispersion, their familiarity with one another, their access to and familiarity with computers and the Internet, and the typical turnover the group may have. Getting more details about their job roles, current performance, challenges, and learning preferences will also help you make better curation decisions.

In later chapters, we will discuss how important self-direction and social learning are to the success of a learning environment. As you explore the characteristics of your learner group, be sure to assess their degree of motivation for learning in the defined arena and the skills they have for managing their own learning. You'll want to identify the kinds of support the environment may need to provide to promote motivation and self-direction. Additionally, you'll need a high-level assessment of the learners' current social learning practices and their readiness to engage with one another and others to support their own learning. It may be important to know how friendly and supportive the work environment is, as well as how much trust and mutual learning is already a part of the group's make up. (See the self-directed learning pillar strength assessment in chapter 3 and the social learning readiness assessment in chapter 4 for additional ideas on what to explore in these areas.)

And of course, you want to develop a more nuanced understanding of the target group's learning needs in relation to the topic. You need to know the degree and nature of their baseline knowledge and skills. Your needs assessment should explore how the learners define their learning needs, as well as their preferences for modes, tools, and techniques for learning.

Solidifying the Topic and Scope

To have a manageable focus for the environment, you have to balance the breadth you cover and the number of contexts in which the learning will be applied. Your decisions here often influence how you envision your core learner group.

You can imagine, for example, that learners in any topic area could have novice, intermediate, or advanced levels of knowledge and skill. If the topic is narrow enough, you may be able to support development at all levels and serve a wide range of people. But it's also possible to focus your attention only on the newcomers, or only on the advanced level practitioners.

Another way of refining topic scope is to consider the context in which your learners will be applying their new knowledge and skills. Because learning is best promoted when it is contextualized, a variety of contexts may increase the scope of what you need to include. Some variability among application contexts is inevitable, of course, but you may need the group to have enough in common that you are not trying to create multiple streams of resources for learners who are in very different contexts.

For example, you might be building an environment that supports the development of presentation skills. It may be reasonable to envision supporting learning from novice to expert; however, it will be difficult to serve all the needs for people who do sales presentations *and* people who report project results *and* people who do keynote presentations in a large venue. Each of these contexts suggests different knowledge and skill needs, and therefore different resources.

Or consider the possibility of building an environment to support writing skills. Depending on your target audience, you may choose to focus only on writing in an academic context (perhaps writing for an academic publication), writing marketing materials, or writing for online publication. Narrowing the focus helps you to have a more reasonable scope. You may also want to narrow the level of writing skills you tackle—deciding, for example, that the environment won't aim to serve those who need help with core grammar skills.

Crafting a Blueprint

You may have noticed that identifying purpose, learner group, context, and so on is not a series of linear steps. Making these decisions is a balancing act that requires an understanding of the impact of each decision on the others. For example, knowing the learner group you want to serve can help you make decisions about topic and scope. On another project, further analysis of the business goals you are trying to support may push you to expand your learner group. There is no one right way to go about finding the right balance, but the business goals and performance context can help anchor your decisions.

Often, creating a blueprint is a two-step process. In the first step, you document the business goals and performance context, your purpose, a description of your learners, and your topic and scope. In the second step, you use your emerging blueprint to enter into additional processes: to find and curate components, and sketch out how they might be assembled. As your vision comes together, you can develop a longer-term plan for cultivating and evolving the environment over time.

FINDING

Finding is locating a range of resources and activities that are on topic. It involves gathering ideas from subject matter experts and learners as well as conducting a search for resources available on the web.

Finding encapsulates these activities:

- gathering current resources
- researching additional resources
- encouraging learners to contribute.

Finding the resources to recommend to your learners is an important part of learning environment design. Learners will almost always attempt to find resources to support their own learning, but this can be an inefficient and frustrating process, especially now that the web offers so many options. Your role is to find valuable, on-point resources; that means finding and curating from a lot of options. The learning environment components chart (see Figure 1-1) is a useful guide to searching for a variety of components.

Gathering Current Resources

Start with the learners and senior people familiar with the knowledge base and skill you are trying to support. Ask them to share any resources they have found useful. (See the suggested focus group agenda sidebar.) Use a blank components chart (or another organization scheme) to capture the results of this initial research. You could also use your time with learners and subject matter experts to explore any areas for which they have been unable to find relevant resources (topics or types) so you can concentrate your energy there.

A Focus Group Method for Gathering Learners' Suggestions for a Learning Environment

One effective method for gathering information about what's already there is to facilitate a focus group. Bring together a small group of learners to discuss how they learn the knowledge and skills you are targeting. Use the components chart as a guide to ask pointed questions to draw out what's available, how effective it is, and what's missing.

The process might look like this:

1. **Focus.** Get the focus group participants to focus on the topic at hand, lay out the knowledge and skills you are targeting, and perhaps generate a short discussion to clarify them.

2. **Free write.** Ask participants to free write (on individual sticky notes) all the resources they use to support their own learning in these areas.

3. **Document.** While they are writing, post component category labels around the room. These could be "resources, people, formal training and education, development practices, experiential learning practices," or they could be categories of your own devising. When participants are finished, briefly explain the categories and ask them to post their ideas in the relevant areas. Provide a handout of the component list to prompt further thought. They can continue to write down any ideas and post them as they come to mind.

4. **Discuss.** Now that a collection of resources is on the wall, facilitate a discussion that gets at the following points:
   - Clarify any items that were posted.
   - Determine the perception of those items' effectiveness.
   - Identify additional resources in each category that participants would find useful.
   - Get recommendations about the kinds of new resources that are most important.

Researching Additional Resources

Once you have explored what learners and tenured employees can share with you, it's time to do some additional research on your own to see what you can add of value. Better still, you could engage a small team of people to help you find the best resources, especially if your command of the topic at hand is limited. Senior practitioners or managers may have a better idea of where to look for resources and which search terms are helpful.

You'll need to put all your Internet search skills to use. Look across all the component categories to find resources in as many as possible. The materials don't need to be evenly distributed, but it is important to have a variety. Here are a few places to start:

- Browse the websites of the professional organizations or journals that serve your learners. Consider posting questions about resources if they have a forum you can use.

- Review conference agendas and industry articles to identify thought leaders, experts, and vendors that are relevant to your learners. Look for ways to connect with these people, resources they have published, or formal learning events they run.

- Review the Twitter streams of thought leaders in the field and explore the nature and source of the resources they are sharing. You may also find additional people you can recommend that your learners follow by examining whom these thought leaders follow.

- Search for any vendors, colleges, or universities that serve your learners; they may have resources or links available on their websites, as well as education programs you could recommend.

- Search for articles and blogs to find people who are writing on your topic area; they may have additional helpful content that you can recommend to your learners.

- Go to Diigo, Delicious, or other public bookmarking sites and find out what people have tagged with keywords in your topic.

- Take your list of potential components to internal and industry leaders; see if reviewing your partial list prompts additional ideas.

Consider asking multiple people to conduct some of these searches. Because search engines and social media aggregators use your history to try to ensure you get relevant content at the top of your search results, different people will get different results (sometimes vastly different results).

Once you know the learners' perceptions about possible learning resources and the usefulness of the materials they mention, you should also do your own evaluation of their quality and effectiveness (see the section on curating in this chapter). Part of the role of curation is to select the most high-quality resources.

Encouraging Learners to Contribute

A learning environment can be made all the richer with the active involvement of the learners themselves. As learners find additional resources they want to recommend to their peers, they should be able to contribute those items, either directly (recommended) or through a vetting process (if necessary). Some of the richest learning environments encourage the learner group to create resources that teach their peers. Providing the software (screen capture or video-making software) or tools (internal blogging or messaging) is one way to encourage learner-generated content.

A big concern of many learning environment sponsors and owners is ensuring that the resources are accurate and of high quality. You could put a process in place that requires all new additions to be vetted (before or soon after being made available), which may be required in a regulated environment. Another strategy is to allow learners to rate the materials or flag materials that are inaccurate, inappropriate, or otherwise not useful.

To learning professionals who pride themselves on the quality and accuracy of their work, giving carte blanche to add resources that have not been proofread or fact-checked may be disturbing. But many who have allowed it (Wikipedia among the most famous) have learned that inaccurate materials are usually quickly identified, either by experts monitoring additions or learners who recognize mistakes. Most people who contribute aim to share good-quality materials. If issues do appear, it's better that they become known in the organization rather than going unrecognized.

Allowing learners to contribute in these ways makes creating and maintaining a curated list of resources much more efficient, which is a nice advantage. Again, determining if and how learners may contribute to the curated list is a judgment call, and there is no one right answer. Still, erring on the side of making the environment as open as possible is recommended because it communicates a degree of trust and respect that is a good message to employees.

CURATING

Curating is using expert judgment to recommend the most relevant and useful components for the learning environment's specific learners and purpose.

Curating encapsulates these activities:

- filtering
- categorizing and tagging
- adding value by contextualizing and highlighting
- making connections and generating discussion.

There is a big difference between aggregation and curation! The curation process requires you to select the best resources among all the possibilities you gathered in the finding process. Curators add value when they perform the following actions:

- **Find** material to keep the collection fresh.
- **Filter** material using human judgment to identify what is relevant and valuable.
- **Categorize and tag** to make the right material easy to find.
- **Contextualize** and add commentary to enrich the impact of the collection.
- **Highlight** trends and bigger-picture stories to enable sense making.
- **Make connections** between related (and seemingly unrelated) materials to provide deeper insight (often through initiating discussions).
- **Generate discussion** among people to create a community and enable knowledge and skill creation.

As you can see from this list of actions, the learning strategist or learning environment leader does much more than simply provide a lot of links. Without the organizing structure, contextualization, and enrichment provided by highlighting, connecting, and enabling discussion, your collection is just one step removed from an Internet search.

Filtering

Harold Rheingold (2012) calls the filtering process "crap detection" and it's a good idea to be skeptical. Your skepticism should extend to any resource or activity you find, not just those on the Internet. There are a few things we can do to filter the materials we find: validate sources, sanity-check using your own expertise, quality-check the materials, and check for copyright.

VALIDATE SOURCES

We all know that anyone can put anything up on the Internet, but there is something about a professional-looking webpage and the solidity of published materials that lessens our inclination to doubt. Depending on your level of concern, there are many strategies that can be used to validate the source of what you are finding. Here are the basics:

- **About:** Check the "about" section or biographies for the relevant credentials of the information's source. You may also want to validate that information through other sources (for example, by checking LinkedIn or employer sites for corroboration). If there isn't an "about" section, backtracking the URL to the primary webpage may give you an indication of the authors.

- **Links:** Check whether credible referrers are linking to a site by searching "link: URL" to see who links to that page (and what they say about it).

- **Investigate the source:** Search for the people and organizations referenced in the material, and look for any news articles, endorsements, or critiques.

- **Check for currency:** Look for copyright dates. If you're looking at a webpage, check to see when the page was posted or last edited. If the content cites other articles or books, what is the most recent date on the list of references? If the topic is evolving, outdated material won't be your best source.

SANITY-CHECK USING YOUR OWN EXPERTISE

Expertise is the primary tool curators use for validating potential resources. If you are not an expert in what you are curating, it is important to recruit a good advisory board or trusted subject matter expert to serve that role. Triangulation (multiple search strategies) or saturation (keep looking until searches start giving results you already have) are also good practices to put into play here—look to see if multiple sources say similar things, and then pick the best one or two in your opinion.

QUALITY-CHECK THE MATERIALS

Consider whether the material meets the standards for quality that your learners expect. Linking to poorly designed websites, clumsily produced videos, or grammatically incorrect articles will call into question the accuracy of the material, as well as the carefulness of your curation. A small lack of production quality is acceptable when the material is otherwise above grade; for example, many great tutorials are produced using smartphone cameras, without fancy lighting or subtitling. Evaluate all aspects of a piece before making a decision. Your quality check may also lead you to recommend revisions to materials that are already available to learners (such as enhancements to your internal database).

All materials should be accurate, timely, engaging, and relevant to the learner's context. Here is some additional advice for checking the quality of different categories of components.

- **Resources:** While they don't need to be perfect, they should be of solid production quality (well-written, clear video and audio, easy to follow). If a resource is a link to a database, that database should be accessible, searchable, and well-categorized; it is often helpful that they be annotated in some way.

- **People:** If you recommend social media connections (blogs and Twitter feeds), look for active accounts with regular posts that are likely to be relevant to learners. Discussion boards should be frequently monitored and easy to filter. (Also check to see if they often post materials not appropriate for work.)

- **Training and education:** Vet training and education recommendations for adherence to endorsed practices and adult learning principles. If possible, include a variety of delivery modes to meet varying learner preferences.

- **Development practices:** High-quality practices are relatively easy to implement and consistent over time.

- **Experiential learning practices:** Tools for self-assessment or suggested reflection questions and exercises should be clear and validated (if possible). Related recommendations for next steps should also be available.

CHECK FOR COPYRIGHT

Check the copyright information or website terms of use for the requirements related to linking to materials or copying them to your own servers. Sometimes, copyright owners request that you link to a webpage, rather than linking directly to a PDF that is on the site. Most people do not allow you to copy their content to your site without permission (which can be free). Some companies may have internal guidelines related to linking to web content, so be sure to check with the appropriate colleagues for additional limits if that is the case.

Filtering is an early step in the curation process, and a valuable one. Once you've validated, sanity-checked, and quality-checked the components you have found (and ensured you have permission to link to them), your list may be somewhat whittled down and you'll be able to make your final selections on what to include in the learning environment. Learners count on you to cut through the noise and find the most useful materials to support their learning. If they find that the material is inaccurate, outdated, or relatively useless, they'll go back to using their own search methodologies for finding materials, and your attempts to support them will be for naught.

> The question is, by what mechanism does the cream rise to the top? The secret ingredient is people. In order to collect the best content and put it together, someone's got to figure out what's best. That's what curators do; they bring their judgment and experience and taste to bear on the question of what you and I should look at next. *And we cannot survive without them.*
>
> —Steven Rosenbaum, *Curation Nation*

Categorizing and Tagging

The curating tasks of categorizing and tagging actually have their biggest impact on the assembling process—when you pull the resources together in some kind of package for the learners. The longer the list of resources, the more important it is that it can be browsed and searched using keywords and categories. Your platform will determine how this looks to your learners, but defining the actual category and keyword terms is an important decision for the curator to make.

In documenting your component list, use ways of categorizing the components that will make sense to the learners and the stakeholders, rather than the component categories. The component categories in the learning environment design framework are useful guidelines from a design perspective, but you'll probably want to use a more custom-ized scheme for communicating to your stakeholders.

Often, the most useful categorization takes into consideration what the learner wants to be able to *to do*, because people search the environ-ment to support their tasks or projects. Using categories that align with the work flow or are action verbs helps learners quickly find what they need. Or, the knowledge base and skill set you are covering may inherently have a topic-specific categorization scheme that learners will understand. Tagging things in multiple categories can also support ease of use (such as by process step and type of resource).

In their work with collating performance support assets, Conrad Gottfredson and Bob Mosher (2011) describe four different kinds of categorization schemes you could consider:

- workflow context: organized by process step
- job role context: organized by who is accountable

- task context: organized by association with specific things to do
- custom context: organized by categories specific to the project.

When considering how to categorize and sort materials, be sure to talk with your learners and gain their perspective. Experts in the topic area may also provide important insights to this part of the process. Where possible, it can be very useful to use "folksonomies"—that is, to allow the learners to tag content in ways that are meaningful to them (or to help name the categories you will use).

The act of categorizing and tagging often reveals weak areas in your learning environment; you'll discover that you may have too much of one category and not enough in another. Your curation process can therefore send you back into finding mode as you seek to deepen those areas you missed in the first round.

Contextualizing and Highlighting

The problem with search results and lists of links is that they often don't give any explanation of why certain things are useful or how to apply the material to your work. Thus, where possible, it can be quite helpful for the designer or curator to point out important material or applications. This can be done using brief descriptions or through clues on the site where the materials are accessed (for example, by featuring content or making its context explicit). While this is only a small aspect of curating, anyone who has tried to find something from an Internet search result will tell you that helping people understand the significance of an item before they click on it is very helpful. The same is true when your materials are in physical space—a wall of books is a daunting sight, but there are many ways to highlight resources for specific purposes.

Making Connections and Generating Discussion

Making connections and generating discussion are advanced functions of the curator role, which especially come into play when the learner group is developing new knowledge or practices. The role isn't played by just one person; instead, any member of the group can point out how ideas connect and get people talking about problems and ideas.

You'll see connections being discussed on blogs associated with the learning environment or on discussion boards. Most importantly, this kind of curation add-on happens in hallway conversations and over lunches—whenever people get together to talk about their work. The learners point each other to additional resources and add in new ideas they've discovered.

Our role as learning environment designers is to ensure that the environment is conducive to these conversations, whether they are happening electronically or in person. See chapter 4 for more on building a learning community.

ASSEMBLING

Assembling is collating and packaging the resources and activities and making them available to your learners.

It encapsulates the following activities:
- determining how learners will access the environment
- incorporating learner-friendly functionality
- envisioning the look and feel
- opening the gates.

Imagine that you have done your research and gathered helpful Internet links, database links, and articles; identified the thought leaders on the topic; vetted conference options; identified courses that might be useful; collated some helpful on-the-job practices; strategized a discussion forum and learner-generated content approach; and more. You have all this curated stuff; where does it go? How do you provide access to these resources and activities?

Determining How Learners Will Access the Environment

Most often, learners access the environment through an electronic portal of some kind. A portal can act as a metaphorical gate to your garden of resources. The trick is to design a portal that is intuitive and flexible. There are a number of tools that promise that capability, including SharePoint, Yammer, Jive, SocialCast, and Canvas. These possibilities all have their limits in terms of ease of use, customizability, and capacities, but—unless you have the capability to design your own portal—they provide the starting point for collating resources and providing an entryway to curated content.

A portal is a great organizing solution for links, resources, and discussion boards, but perhaps less so for accessing people, development practices, and learning by doing. Still, an expert directory, articles or resources for establishing development practices, and advice on improving your on-the-job learning can be useful. Even resources on learning to learn can be highly valuable, and can be included on a portal.

It's possible that creating a portal doesn't really make sense, perhaps because your learners are using tools that are difficult to collate, or the components just don't need to be organized in one entry point. Some projects can be "assembled" by simply providing a short job aid that provides links and guidance for learners to set up their own personal learning environments. And if a one-stop portal isn't possible in your organization because of regulatory, budgetary, or system constraints, an old-fashioned resource handbook can work just fine.

Incorporating Learner-Friendly Functionality

Whatever you create, you want to check that you've met ease-of-use criteria to make sure it is inviting to learners. The learning environment should have some of the following characteristics, given the purpose, type, and platform of your environment:

- **Easily accessed in the normal flow of work:** The environment should be accessible to learners at the point of need.
- **Searchable:** Learners need to be able to quickly locate what they need.
- **Intuitively organized:** The organization scheme should use categories and tags that learners recognize.
- **Up-to-date:** Outdated material should be removed regularly.
- **Annotated:** Each item should contain a brief description to help learners know if it's what they're looking for before they get too deep.
- **Tagable:** Where possible, allow learners to tag or save their favorite resources.

- **Rateable:** Learners should be able to highlight the most useful resources for their peers (and identify questionable resources for learning environment leaders).

- **Open:** Learners and experts should have some mechanism to contribute resources and activities to the environment.

- **Visually appealing:** The site should convey energy and appear uncluttered, organized, and modern.

If the nature of your learning environment doesn't incorporate an online portal, some of these ease-of-use criteria can still be applied. Any documentation still needs to be easily accessed, searchable, intuitively organized, up-to-date, and annotated to some degree.

Envisioning the Look and Feel

However you communicate your learning environment to your learners, it should have a look and feel that conveys value, credibility, energy, and ease of use. As you get ready to assemble the environment, determine a visual and graphic design that is professional and appealing. Don't underestimate the importance of the visual design of the documents or webpages you use to provide access to materials; similarly, don't underestimate the importance of the comfort and decorating scheme of physical environments.

Visual cues help learners feel confident and excited about using the learning environment. Anyone with experience using computers has an appreciation of the way that user interface design can support the use of a system or make it frustrating and time-consuming.

Research has now proven that multimedia and interface design affects how users learn. The myth of visual design as an optional extra (which is alive in too many dark corners) is in desperate need of busting. The hard fact is that how you create graphics, sequence interaction, display information, use animation, and design for social presence and emotion will impact how users learn. This is interface design.

—Dorian Peters, *Interface Design for Learning*

At a high level, you'll need to pay attention to the use of graphics and animation, as well as colors, typefaces, and layout. Equally important are your decisions about information design and architecture: the structure of the site, labels used, and navigation.

Dorian Peters has written a well-researched book, *Interface Design for Learning,* which is a fantastic manual for the nuances of creating an effective look and feel for your learning environment. Another great resource is Connie Malamed's *Visual Design Solutions.* In many organizations, you will collaborate with other experts in information technology or web design, but interface and visual design for learning have additional requirements based on learning theory concepts, such as cognitive load and scaffolding.

Opening the Gates

Once the learning environment is assembled, it's time to open the gates and invite the learners in. When launching an environment, it's often helpful to have a full-scale publicity campaign and some special events that call attention to the resources available. Here are some of the ways that you can actively invite your learners to take advantage of (and contribute to) the environment:

- Publicize the learning environment through some of the same channels you publicize your formal learning events (email, web banners).

- Arrange demonstrations for learners, which could take the form of a table in the lunchroom, a video on the homepage, or a presentation at a staff meeting.

- Invite supervisors and informal leaders to be advocates for the environment.

- Begin compelling conversations on the environment's discussion boards or social media streams to demonstrate the value of asynchronous exchanges on topics of interest.

- If you have options for learners to contribute, host "seeding" events that ask people to contribute resources for specific subtopics or resources of a particular type.

- Share wins from the social interaction aspects of your learning environment to show examples that others might imitate.

- When new people come on board, be sure to formally orient them to the learning environment. New hire training programs should use the learning environment as much as possible to demonstrate to learners how to find resources and support their ongoing development.

In a world full of distractions and new tools, it's never enough to simply publicize the opening of your environment. Your cultivation plan should include ongoing communication and intermittent publicity efforts. Once the learners fully engage with the environment and make it their own, you may be able to pull back, but you can boost learners' efforts with continued promotion. Consider regularly repeating some of the strategies you employed to launch the environment. Of course, the most impactful publicity is always word-of-mouth, and the more your learners find ongoing value and support in the learning environment, the more they will engage with it, contribute to it, and tell their peers about it.

CULTIVATING

Cultivating is the process of ensuring that the environment continues to be fresh, enticing, and useful, which requires the infusion of new material, pruning of outdated resources, and ongoing evaluation of what's working and not working.

Cultivating encapsulates the following activities:

- establishing leadership for the environment
- expanding and improving the environment over time
- nurturing a learning community
- pruning and keeping the environment fresh
- evaluating the learning environment.

Any gardener will assure you that planting is just the beginning of an ongoing cultivation process as the garden evolves. The same is true of a learning environment.

A vibrant environment lives and breathes, and you have to plan for how it is going to grow and the roles and resources needed to keep it flourishing. Instituting an annual or semiannual comprehensive review would be a good practice, because it ensures some concerted attention on cultivating the environment on a regular basis. (Some projects might even justify a quarterly review if the topic is evolving rapidly.)

Just like a beautiful garden choked with weeds, an untended learning environment stops being useful, and all the work you did in assembling and promoting it will have been wasted.

Establishing Leadership for the Environment

One of your most important tasks is to establish leadership of the environment by some invested party: a steering committee, management team, or senior practitioner. You should do this early in the learning environment design process, while you are still finding and curating potential resources. Leaders must value the environment and understand the current work context, as well as the emerging knowledge and skill development needs.

The role of leaders is to continuously oversee the environment and ensure that it is achieving its purpose. They may vet additional materials and activities that are added, serve as social media authors (for blogs and Twitter feeds), act as advocates in the workplace, commit to responding to discussion board questions, and so on. They may also identify and commission new resources to meet emerging needs. In the most active environments, the leadership role is often taken over by the learners themselves. Nonetheless, designating someone to keep an eye on the activity and outcomes is wise.

It is important to communicate that ongoing evaluation, maintenance, and enhancement activities will need to be supported over time. Estimate the amount of time that may be necessary—this will depend on the nature of the environment and the role you have assigned to leaders—and make sure that leaders have enough time to do the work. This time must also be protected; otherwise newer projects or pressing deadlines will cause needed cultivation to fall by the wayside. Consider having leaders track their time so you can better manage it. You may also need to develop high-level plans for learner-generated content and its ongoing cultivation in order to give your stakeholders a realistic view of what this part of the process will entail. These plans are often part of the learning environment blueprint.

Expanding and Improving the Environment Over Time

The leaders and designers of the environment should continue to actively identify new resources. They should also monitor the knowledge and skill base of the learners, as well as their performance demands and business goals, so that evolving needs can be addressed. The owners and designers can support ongoing learning through exemplary curation practices—especially by highlighting, making connections, and generating relevant discussions in order to make the environment an active learning resource center.

An important mechanism for cultivating a learning environment is the involvement of the learners themselves. Many environments incorporate a strategy for learner-generated content, by which the learners can suggest or add resources to the mix. Some organizations provide tools for people to create their own resources (such as short videos or screencasts) so that they can share their knowledge and skills with one another. There are potential drawbacks to this method; with many contributors, each with their own way of thinking about the subject, it's easy for your "curated" materials to grow into a mountain of resources in which it is impossible to find what you need.

Nurturing a Learning Community

Promoting interaction among learners and between learners and experts is often at the heart of a learning environment, and it usually requires more effort than just opening up social spaces. Tactics for nurturing a community are discussed in chapter 4 and you'll find many specific considerations and ideas on those pages. At a high level, nurturing a learning community involves facilitating engagement among members, prompting contributions to the site through learner-generated content or participation in discussions, ensuring timely responses, inviting experts to engage, promoting successes, deliberately starting interesting conversations, addressing emerging needs, moderating experience, cultivating support for the environment, and reporting on results and outcomes.

Some environments may need little intervention to promote interaction, whereas others may need some help to get started. You can't make people engage (and you shouldn't require it); your role is to make the environment so useful and enticing that people willingly leverage it for their own learning.

Pruning and Keeping the Environment Fresh

While the environment grows, it's also critical that you weed out any resources that become outdated or prove to be unpopular with learners.

This, again, is where the curator role comes in. A curator must be a tough critic and a ruthless pruner, making some materials unavailable so that the best can stand out. Don't underestimate how important this part of the curating role is; your intent is to provide a narrower set of options that have been well vetted, not to duplicate what can be found through a search engine. Very little actually gets thrown away, but learners who want more obscure resources may need to go into an archives section to find what they are looking for.

To guide pruning, environments can enable rating systems or comments and suggestions that allow learners to identify the best resources and those that are not particularly helpful. Some resources may be tagged with expiration dates so they are automatically removed or sent for review.

An important consideration while you are curating and pruning is attending to the diversity of the available materials. Curating materials means you are narrowing your learners' fields of vision, but it is also important to have diversity of thought and resources in order to support deeper thinking and innovative application. Giving learners multiple approaches to a skill or several articles on a particular point increases the likelihood that they will find relatable material. Hiving diverse content is a delicate balancing act because you don't want to confuse learners with too many options and approaches. Being transparent in the decisions you make can help stakeholders weigh in if needed.

Evaluating the Learning Environment

In the age of big data it is important to determine which data will serve you well in ensuring that the environment effectively supports the intended knowledge and skill development. The key questions you want to ask are:

- To what degree is the learning environment fulfilling its purpose?

- To what degree are learners able to find what they need to support their own learning and development goals? (What's missing? What is hard to find?)

- Which resources are most useful, and which need to be removed?

- To what degree are learners improving in their knowledge, skill, and capability on the job in the targeted areas? To what degree is the learning environment supportive of this improvement?

- To what degree is growing capability in the targeted knowledge or skill area evident in the performance of the learners on the job?

The most valuable data help you continue to make decisions to keep the environment active and fresh. Computer-based systems often provide access data (how many people have clicked on a resource) and other indicators of use, but these data aren't necessarily indicative of the content's quality or usefulness, and are not recommended for decision making (see the first column of Table 2-2). More helpful data are those that indicate how useful the resources are (as rated by users). If you can enable a rating system of some kind, that data will make it more efficient to identify components that need improvement or pruning.

You may also have formal quality evaluation strategies for some of your components (for example, course evaluation practices and feedback forms). Informal observation data could also be gathered from development practices and what managers can see of experiential learning practices. These data points help to evaluate specific components, but not the learning environment as a whole.

Table 2-2 illustrates further ways to evaluate the learning environment.

TABLE 2-2. POTENTIAL LEARNING ENVIRONMENT MEASURES

Activity	Value	Impact
(Not recommended for decision making) • Page views / access • Posts and comments • Attendance • Contribution rates • Self-report of activity (survey)	• Q&A activity • Response timeliness • Return visitors • Referrals • Ratings • Learner evaluations • Feedback	• Learner evaluations • Learner behavior change • Manager evaluations • Use cases • Success stories • Performance indicators • Business outcomes

The most efficient and credible approaches to evaluating learning environments as a whole are survey and focus group data. Short surveys can be sent to entire learning groups and their managers to gather data on the questions outlined. Focus groups can provide richer perspectives and more nuanced feedback. These strategies can be accomplished efficiently and will aid in decision making about the learning environment strategy.

It is also critically important to keep your eye on the reason the learning environment was called for in the first place—the business and performance goals that required the capability being developed. Even if people rave about your environment, you still need to monitor the business and performance indicators. If they are not where they need to be, you'll want to analyze whether the environment is addressing the right needs, or if there are other learning-related or performance environment problems that need to be tackled. While we may want to bask in strong evaluations from learners, we (and many of our stakeholders) are more interested in evaluating the outcomes.

PROJECT MANAGEMENT

Managing the design and development of a learning environment is often a multifaceted task, and it's useful to think of it like a software product (version 1, 1.1, 1.2, and so forth) rather than as a defined project that will be closed out immediately after launch. There will no doubt be iterations, additions, and occasional fixes, even after the environment has been made available to your learners.

In addition to managing the ongoing development of the environment, you may also launch specific custom design, development, and implementation projects. Perhaps you determine that you need a database that doesn't yet exist, or that existing training needs some additional modules. Your ongoing plan may also include a regularly published blog, newsletters, or Twitter feed, and you might need to manage authors and posting schedules.

Your overall process could also involve prioritizing what needs to be created or revised, and launching separate design projects for these components. Your envisioning and project management skills will come into play as you think of the full scope of the environment you plan to craft, while juggling all the tasks needed to complete desired components.

At some point, you will have enough material in place to launch, even if you are still building or researching some components. Don't let a lack of some resources keep you from doing this. Learning environment design is a long-term effort; a project that is never "done." Go ahead and launch the environment as a work-in-progress, so long as there is some obvious value to what you already have. The more you can demonstrate the value of the environment for the learners and for the accomplishment of business goals and initiatives, the more support you will have for developing additional components.

Ongoing management also includes additional curation, regular pruning, evaluation, and ongoing communication. These tasks are part of the management of the environment. For some environments, these tasks will be relatively easy, whereas others may need a near full-time manager or a small team of owners to oversee these processes and build community. Every project will have its own requirements and challenges, and you would be wise to bring your project management skills to the table along with your ability to envision the possibilities that a learning environment strategy will enable.

HIGH-LEVEL ENVIRONMENT QUALITY CHECK

There are no hard-and-fast rules about creating a "perfect" arrangement of resources and activities. Just as a gardener is constantly acquiring new plantings and exhibiting them in different configurations, a learning environment designer or owner is always actively curating the collection. These processes are recurring constantly or regularly in order to keep up with the changing needs of learners and emerging knowledge and skill advances in their fields.

Nonetheless, there are some broad quality checks you can apply to your environment-in-progress to assess its likelihood to be useful.

- Validate that you have the materials that will help you achieve your purpose. Put yourself in the learners' shoes and imagine what you would need to embark on self-directed development in their contexts. (Or work with a subgroup of learners to validate your recommendations.)

- Ensure that there are resources across all component categories, although it is not necessary to have an equal number in each. In some instances you may have little control over development practices; in those cases, you might consider adding a set of resources to help managers establish development practices within their organizations or teams.

- Verify that the environment has elements that promote learner motivation and self-direction. This characteristic of your environment is usually supported by materials in every category.

- Review resources and activities with an eye toward the degree of learner engagement they promote. Are there plenty of components that can be described as enticing, interesting, challenging, provocative, hands-on, or interactive?

- Be sure you have elements that promote learning by doing. Most importantly, ensure that the environment supports experimentation, feedback, and reflection.

- Consider Conrad Gottfredson and Bob Mosher's "five moments of need"—the idea that employees need support on five broad occasions: when they want to learn for the first time, when they want to expand or enrich their learning in an arena, when they apply their learning, when things change, and when things go wrong (2011). Imagine your learners in any of these situations and see if you have resources that would help.

You can do additional quality checks at the component level. This chapter contained specific recommendations about filtering and curating materials that should prove useful; in addition, you may have your own criteria.

The job of curating an environment is a big one, and it is important to underscore how vital it is to continue to curate on an ongoing basis. Learning environment design is not a once-and-done project; it requires consistent attention from people who are vested in continuing to support the learners in their development.

PRINCIPLES OF LEARNING ENVIRONMENT DESIGN

Learning environment design is often very emergent, being put together over time by those committed to supporting development—whether designers, learning leaders, or learners themselves. There is no one right way of designing a learning environment, but there are some essential principles that can provide broad guidance to whatever activities take place to curate and assemble an environment. The following are some essential principles for designing learning environments:

- **Empower and trust learners:** Assume that learners are capable of identifying their own needs and following through to learn and apply (even if you need to provide some initial scaffolding for their efforts). If you try to encourage activity by requiring participation, you'll likely cause more harm than good to your learning environment. Work on establishing expectations for learning and performance, promoting learner motivation by pointing out benefits, and engaging exemplary learners. Empower learners to select and access materials when they need them. Then trust that the learners can take it from there.

- **Focus on context:** Focus on what learners need to be able to do in context, not just on what they need to know. Adults organize what they are learning primarily on the basis of what it helps them to do. Learning content in a vacuum is often frustrating and confusing. It's always important to invite learners to imagine where they will apply their learning as they begin.

- **Curate effectively:** Curate materials that are the most relevant, reflect quality characteristics, and are likely to appeal to learners. Recommending high-quality learning resources is a huge value for people who need access to materials just in time, and is the whole point of learning environment design.

- **Provide variety and depth:** Because we don't always know what learners will bring to the table or exactly how they will apply the learning, the chance of having relevant resources is increased when the resources are varied (within the scope of the vision). Even within a unifying purpose, you can have many differences—in angles on a topic, points of view represented, preferences for learning materials (text-based or video), levels of depth (novice, intermediate, or expert), and so on. The environment will be most valued when it continues to be useful even as learners actively develop their knowledge base and skills.

- **Make access easy:** Make resources easy to find and access, both electronically and person-to-person. Avoid aggregating resources in a list that is little better than the first pages of a browser search—just a jumble in which it is difficult to find what you need.

CONCLUDING THOUGHTS

As this chapter has conveyed, the processes of learning environment design are multifaceted and iterative. While they may seem complex, they don't have to be over engineered. Done well, your efforts to ensuring that learners have access to a robust learning environment for their ongoing development needs will be highly valued.

The beauty of a learning environment is that it can grow over time, just like a lovely garden. Start with the essential pieces and add additional components as time allows (with the help of learners and subject matter experts, if possible). Notice what learners use and what they seem to be missing, and respond accordingly. Keep in close touch so you can anticipate changes in their needs and monitor the effectiveness of the curated resources.

Some learning environments may become unnecessary, but most can gradually change and evolve—simply becoming more rich and valuable over time. The processes of learning environment design can help you lay a good foundation and continuously improve the environments you assemble.

3

Motivation and Self-Direction

Learning environments give learners a great deal of freedom and control to manage their own learning. They can access performance support as they need it, get quick skill pointers in the flow of work, pop up from their desks to consult with a colleague, and access all manner of resources and activities for ongoing development. Learners determine what they want to learn, which resources and approaches they want to access in order to learn, when to engage in learning activities, and how and where they are going to apply their learning.

In contemporary workplaces, this is exactly what is required. We have come to understand that many learning needs do not require formal solutions; in fact, formal solutions can be a waste of time. In *The Power of Pull* from the Deloitte Centre for the Edge, John Hagel, John Seely Brown, and Lang Davison have suggested that informal learning is necessary in the workplace because the knowledge and skills that people need to be effective are continuously emerging. By the time knowledge is captured and repackaged for formal training, it's out of date. New knowledge and skills often need to be developed in the flow of work. These thought leaders assert that successful workers will be the ones who develop an exceptional ability to pull information as needed and share knowledge and skills as they emerge.

It's a powerful vision, and one that needs to inform our approach to supporting learning in the workplace. But there is a caution. This kind of self-provisioned, in-the-workflow learning requires learners to have specific learning skills, and many employees do not know how to learn in this fashion. Many are accustomed to getting guidance from teachers, trainers, and coaches; they may not have developed the capabilities that lead to self-directed learning success. They may not even recognize that they don't employ effective learning skills. A 2014 CEB study found that only 20 percent of learners were engaging in effective learning strategies.

It is important to note, then, that the foundational element on the learning environment chart is learner motivation and self-direction; it underpins the ability to take advantage of every component in the environment, including formal training and education. If that element is weak—if employees lack motivation or are unskilled at managing their own learning—a learning environment strategy may fail.

So while a learning environment strategy fits in with a futuristic vision, some employees may not be quite ready to take advantage of a set of materials and activities for self-directed learning. This does not imply, however, that learning needs to be controlled and monitored. Instead, learning leaders can incorporate a number of supports into the learning environment that smooth the way for learners who are not used to these more informal and in-the-moment approaches.

To be effective at designing a learning environment and promoting a productive learning culture, designers should understand the capabilities necessary for effective self-directed learning, and they should reorient some of their design skills toward building learning capability in the workforce.

Motivation and self-direction are as important to the success of a learning environment as sunlight is to the growth of a garden.

SELF-DIRECTED LEARNING PILLARS

Learner motivation and self-directed learning have been topics for research and theorizing for decades, and many useful models and recommendations have come out of those studies. According to the research, adults who engage in self-directed learning start with a recognition of a discrepancy between expectations and reality, or a recognition of a need to learn. This prompts an individual to analyze and identify the knowledge and skills needed to move forward. Once needs are identified, self-directed learners usually access and use whatever is most convenient in their immediate surroundings as sources for learning. People are often a go-to option; learners ask questions, seek experts, and ask for recommendations. The digital world has greatly expanded what may be quickly available, but it also provides such an array of choices that learners tend to choose from among only the first few things they encounter. In making their selections, learners look for relevant resources that capture their interest and prove most useful. They often judge the quality of the learning resources on how engaging they are, and how specifically relevant they are to their own context. If there is too much of a leap between the content and the application, learners may miss the connections.

Learners go further afield only when their needs can't be adequately satisfied with at-hand resources. You can imagine, then, why providing curated resources in a learning environment would be a boon. Self-directed learning processes also involve some degree of self-monitoring, because the learners determine the degree to which they have learned from the material they access. And while learners often attempt to learn in the middle of the flow of work, it is helpful for them to pause work in order to engage with learning resources and activities and to process what they are learning.

A synthesis of articles and books on self-directed learning (and other research on successful learning attitudes and skills) suggests a number of key factors that need to be inherent in any effective learning environment: motivation, intention, attention, self-awareness, engagement, relationships, and space and time. These might be considered the seven pillars of self-directed learning (Figure 3-1).

Motivation

People pursue self-directed learning when they are motivated to do so, primarily because they have noted some gap in their knowledge or skills related to things they want to do. In the workplace, people are motivated to learn in order to:

- Attain increased job competence.
- Improve potential for career growth.
- Make progress on a goal.
- Support a cause.
- Avoid failure.
- Belong or be part of something.
- Demonstrate autonomy and independence.
- Meet a challenge.
- Gain stature or respect.
- Attain a desirous lifestyle.

FIGURE 3-1. SELF-DIRECTED LEARNING PILLARS

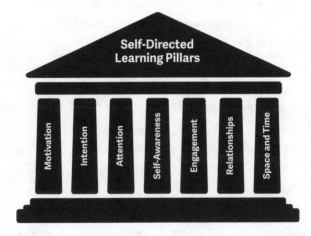

People are motivated because they believe learning will help them do something that will produce an outcome they value. Learners may unconsciously (or consciously) ask themselves: Can I learn this? If I do, what will it get me? Do I value what it will get me?

When you are gathering information about your learners, it's important to get a sense of the degree of motivation they have toward learning the knowledge and skills that are at the center of the learning environment you are designing. If you are concerned that their motivation is weak (or may be overpowered by motivation toward other goals), then a first task is to determine what (if anything) you can do to increase learner motivation (in a positive way).

Learner motivation theorists tell us there are ways facilitators can promote learner motivation and persistence. Tactics include ensuring the relevance of the material, pointing out the real benefits of learning (what learners will be able to do as a result), helping learners feel like they are part of a community, and respecting the learners' experience, contributions, and intelligence (Wlodkowski 2008). Not surprisingly, these are some of the same factors that come up as important to self-directed learning.

Intention

Intention drives learning, and more importantly, it drives the application of learning to specific tasks and roles. Intention is similar to motivation, but much more specific—it's about having explicit objectives with an application context in mind. Learning is deeper and longer lasting when people consider where they can apply the learning while also engaging in learning activities.

Intention is focused by an understanding of how the learning is relevant to achieving goals and accomplishing tasks. The more context-specific and relevant materials are, the more likely that learners will see exactly how their new knowledge can be applied. Transfer of learning research suggests that managers can play a role in promoting intention by helping employees recognize the connection between knowledge and skill development and work achievements (Burke and Hutchins 2007). They can help learners set goals, and they can follow up to support application.

Attention

In a world full of distractions, attention has become a precious commodity. We mislead ourselves into thinking that multitasking makes us more efficient. However, studies have shown that multitasking, which is an act of constantly switching attention, tends to degrade the quality of the attention we are giving to each task.

People need to pay attention in order to learn, and they need to be able to determine exactly what they are supposed to notice or discern. Learning from others requires us to carefully observe specific behaviors and notice the ways in which our behaviors are the same or different; grasping meaning requires us to read and listen closely, taking in the entire message and drilling down on the important parts. Focus, concentration, attentiveness, and vigilance often play a role in learning, and these are qualities that need to be nurtured and developed.

In self-directed learning people have to decide where their attention will be focused, which often requires a longer-term commitment to seeking specific opportunities to learn more about the targeted knowledge base or skill.

Self-Awareness

Knowing one's self—strengths and opportunities—is often a precondition for learning. The process of self-directed learning typically begins with recognizing a gap in a knowledge base or skill (which is needed for current responsibilities or anticipated for future roles or tasks). Identifying these development needs is an exercise in self-analysis and sets the stage for motivation, attention, and intention.

Later in the process, as learners apply their new knowledge or skills, they often need to monitor whether their actions are producing the desired impact or are in alignment with the image in their minds. The critical processes here are reflection and feedback, which further inform and deepen self-knowledge. Learners need tools for self-assessment and models for comparison in order to deepen their self-awareness. They also need the capacity to receive and interpret feedback.

Engagement

To learn, people need to be actively involved in the process, either intellectually or physically (or both). Emotional engagement also promotes learning by adding extra intensity to the experience. Only active engagement can power the brain processes that allow people to retain knowledge and skill.

Engagement is certainly facilitated through experiential learning practices, but other components in the environment are more effective when they are engaging as well. You can engage people through effective writing and solid design skills that ensure that material is interesting, compelling, and memorable. Readings that are emotionally resonant, people who tell great stories, team practices that are highly productive and bonding are all examples of how all kinds of learning activities can be engaging.

Instructional designers, in particular, have developed many strategies to engage learners, which include giving them relevant challenges, letting them see their own progress through repeated practice, minimizing passive activities like reading and listening, and providing frequent opportunities to interact in a variety of intellectually challenging ways (not clicks or movement without learning purpose). Gamification techniques have also been shown to increase engagement in learning. These techniques include crafting learning around a story, introducing challenge and mystery, rewarding learners with advancing levels, ensuring intrinsic and contextual feedback, and giving learners the opportunity to repeat practice in order to get better (Kapp 2012).

Relationships

While we think of self-directed learning as being an independent activity, the truth is that a complete learning process often relies on trusted relationships—people who provide feedback, point out resources, act as role models, and discuss problems. Relationships may be relatively casual (following people on social media) or quite deep (relationships with supportive mentors). We learn from others through questioning, instruction, coaching, observation, reflection, storytelling, and more.

It's important that every learning environment identifies people who can engage with learners as subject matter experts, facilitators of learning, or fellow learners and collaborators. Learners need to have a diversity of perspectives to widen their points of view, and developing trusted relationships is a boon to deeper learning.

Space and Time

It has become common to say that we learn in the flow of work, and some learning through experience is indeed impossible to separate from work. But the kind of development for which you would consider creating a learning environment is usually development that takes time. Not only do learners need to persist in engaging a variety of learning components over time, they also need the head space to reflect, study, and make plans.

When employees worry that they don't have time to learn, it's possible that one of the problems is that they don't have time to waste looking for learning resources. Your work in curating a learning environment provides substantial help in this regard. By minimizing the time spent trying to identify materials and activities to support learning, employees are able to maximize the time they have to dedicate to productive learning.

If your identified learner group is not encouraged (or able) to take time out to reflect and learn, to engage with one another to think over problems, or to take breaks that allow creative energies to recharge, then a learning environment may not be helpful to them. When schedules are tightly packed and employees are required to be engaged in the work nearly every hour of the day, time for learning is hard to find. They may learn from doing the work, of course, but some of their learning goals no doubt require time to engage and process. When workspaces are distracting, concentration may be compromised. While it is often advised to let learners choose their time and place for learning, sometimes clearly allocating time and space is the best support you can provide. This may be especially important in jobs that have no natural lulls, such as call centers and manufacturing.

SHORING UP SELF-DIRECTED LEARNING PILLARS

You can get a sense of how strong and stable the pillars for self-directed learning are among your learner group by considering the quick assessment in Worksheet 3-1.

Be cautious about giving the assessment directly to learners in a survey because it may be hard for them to self-assess some items (they may not have the background to know) and it may be difficult to admit disagreement with some items. You may know the learner group enough to make an estimate, or you can ask your project sponsors and subject matter experts to help.

If fewer than 60 percent of your learners would agree with a particular statement, then it is probably important to do something deliberate to strengthen that pillar. While what you can do is dependent on your learners and context, you may get some ideas from the short list of recommendations in Table 3-1.

WORKSHEET 3-1: PILLAR STRENGTH ASSESSMENT

What percentage of your learners would agree with the following statements related to learning the knowledge and skill area you want to support?

Respond with one of these ranges: 0%, 1-19%, 20-39%, 40-59%, 60-79%, 80-99%, 100%.

Percent Who Would Agree	Statement	Pillar
	Learning in this area is important to me.	Motivation
	I can name specific knowledge and skill areas in this topic about which I am interested in learning more.	Motivation
	When I am learning knowledge and skills in this area, I know where and how I am going to apply that learning.	Intention
	Learning this knowledge base and skill set is relevant to something I need now or in the near future.	Intention
	I know how the learning resources and experiences being offered are relevant to my success.	Attention
	I have a sense of what to focus on when I am learning in this area.	Attention
	I know my own strengths and weaknesses in this knowledge base or skill set.	Self-Awareness
	I am able to identify my own learning goals in this area.	Self-Awareness
	When I am learning in this area, I really get into the flow of the material and am able to focus.	Engagement
	The learning materials and activities that are available to help me build this knowledge base or skill set are relevant, interesting, interactive, and memorable.	Engagement
	It's easy to find people to help me to learn specific knowledge and to develop skills in this area.	Relationships
	I have developed (or am able to develop) relationships with others who support my development.	Relationships
	I can find distraction-free places when I need to focus on learning.	Space and Time
	I have time to pursue learning in this area.	Space and Time
	Generally speaking, I know how to pursue learning when I need it.	General Self-Directedness

This assessment is not meant to be a validated indicator of learning pillar stability, but it can help you analyze whether your learners are ready to manage their own learning.

TABLE 3-1. TACTICS FOR STRENGTHENING MOTIVATION
AND SELF-DIRECTION

To Strengthen This Pillar	Try These Tactics
Motivation	• Draw connections between knowledge, skills, work tasks, and success. • Enlist the support of formal and informal leaders to actively promote importance.
Intention	• Categorize resources by what people might be trying to do. • Select resources that are specifically relevant to the learner's role or industry. • Suggest next steps when an activity is concluded. • Provide application suggestions and exercises. • Use contextualized examples, role plays, and simulations.
Attention	• Point out what can be learned from specific activities and resources. • Advise learners on specific formal learning events for a given stage in their development. • Suggest reflection questions for readings and activities. • Seek out resources in the learners' preferred formats (e.g., videos, podcasts, books, articles). • Provide different views of materials, depending on the learner's role or level of experience.
Self-Awareness	• Provide self-assessment tools with recommended next steps.
Engagement	• Select resources and activities based on how engaging they are. • Ensure that at least a subset of resources and activities provide deep interaction and interpersonal communication. • Take an active role to generate discussion online.

TABLE 3-1. (CONTINUED)

To Strengthen This Pillar	Try These Tactics
Relationships	• Introduce learners to subject matter experts or each other. • Identify people to follow on social media, and suggest specific social media tools, shared repositories, and hashtags. • Recommend professional organizations and conferences. • Provide an expert directory. • Enable profile pages that give learners the chance to share both descriptive information and a little of their personalities. • Offer guidance to ensure that developer-learner pairs have effective interactions with each other.
Space and Time	• Incorporate resources into systems that employees need to do the work (integrated performance support). • Create a resource portal to make searching for resources more efficient. • Allocate sufficient time for learning when needed.
General Self-Directedness	• Create checklists and activity guides. • Offer resources for learning to learn.

DESIGN TOOLS FOR LEARNER MOTIVATION AND SELF-DIRECTION

When learners are deeply self-directive, they are fully capable of managing their choices in a robust learning environment. If your learners are capable of self-direction, but not necessarily experienced at it, then you might want to provide some scaffolding in your environment to help guide them along. Rather than simply hoping for the best, a learning environment designer can apply specific design tools that amplify learner motivation and self-direction: curating, contextualizing, connecting, scaffolding, mapping, and assembling.

Curating involves applying judgment to ensure that the materials included in a learning environment are relevant and high quality. Curation also includes looking for the specific types of materials you have ascertained will be most welcome and useful for your learners. Effective curation supports the pillars of *attention, engagement,* and *motivation.* For more detail, see chapter 2.

Contextualizing means taking action to point out the relevance of the resources available in the environment and to highlight the ways that learning can be applied. Contextualizing is especially helpful for strengthening *intention,* and also supports *attention* and *motivation.* Contextualizing is part of the curation process in learning environment design.

Connecting encompasses all the ways the environment promotes social learning. Actively connecting people strengthens the *relationship* pillar, and often provides a strong support for learner *motivation.* Connecting is what the people component is all about.

Scaffolding involves giving learners active support for completing learning processes. It is a way of strengthening most pillars, but is vital for *self-awareness, attention, intention,* and *space and time.*

Mapping provides specific direction for building a knowledge base or skill—organizing a series of learning activities for maximum impact. A map can be like travel directions, suggesting a specific order for engaging a series of activities. Or it can be more like a sightseeing guide, pointing out not-to-be-missed highlights that can be accessed in any order. Mapping props up *motivation* by giving learners a sense of progress and it supports *attention* by pointing out exactly why each piece is on the map. Often, learners are also given *space and time* to complete a map of learning activities.

Assembling is the process that organizes all the learning materials and resources in an accessible place. The format of the access point (webpages or resource list, for example) helps to focus learners' *attention,* and it saves them wasted time looking for resources.

CONCLUDING THOUGHTS

To say we should support self-directed learning sounds like an oxymoron, doesn't it? There has also been talk of formalizing informal learning, which seems equally contradictory. But a strategy that counts on self-directed learning does not necessarily require learning leaders to step back and leave learners to their own devices. We can endorse "agency"—learners' capacity to act, make choices, and define and satisfy their own learning needs—without abandoning them to the quirks of a browser search. Recognizing the depth of potential resources on the Internet and the irreplaceable personal support obtained from peers and experts does not necessarily mean that we must therefore discontinue providing active support for learning.

> Traditional approaches to learning are no longer capable of coping with a constantly changing world. They have yet to find a balance between the structure that educational institutions provide and the freedom afforded by the new media's almost unlimited resources, without losing a sense of purpose and direction.... Simply unleashing students on the Internet doesn't solve the problem.... The challenge is to find a way to marry structure and freedom to create something altogether new.
>
> —Doug Thomas and John Seely Brown, *A New Culture of Learning*

Jane Hart, Randy Emelo, and others in the field have advocated for learning professionals to become learning coaches and one-on-one advisers, but that model is not scalable in many situations. Learning environment design provides the strategy to "marry structure and freedom to create something altogether new" (Thomas and Seely Brown 2011). It provides direction and support without forcing learners through a specific path or timetable that isn't right for them.

Many of our educational institutions are still using 20th-century teaching strategies, so professionals in the workplace and in institutions of higher education are schooled in more passive, compliance-based approaches to learning. Supporting the development of self-directed learning skills will set learners up for a lifetime of acquiring new knowledge. The energy you may put into shoring up the self-directed learning pillars to enable a learning environment strategy will pay off when learners take those skills and apply them to their next learning need.

4

Supporting a Learning Community

From our earliest moments in life, we learn how to act in the world from interacting with other people. While it can be tempting to focus on available anytime resources to support learning, people report that their most impactful and significant learning comes from exchanges with other people—by watching, conversing, and collaborating with others.

When designing a learning environment, it's important to ask: How can I connect learners to one another? Who are the more advanced practitioners that learners can emulate or learn from? How can we promote interaction for learning purposes?

Research shows that there is a wide range of interpersonal activities that result in learning and performance outcomes (for a review, see Lombardozzi 2013). Scholars parse out different kinds of relational learning; they study intense one-on-one relationships (mentoring, developmental relationships), communities (communities of practice, communities of inquiry), work teams, or coaching relationships, and their studies draw conclusions about each particular context. There are established theories related to social learning, teaching, mentoring, communities of practice, and more, but taken together, these literature streams provide a strong base for understanding in more general terms how people learn through their relationships with others. These ideas can help learning leaders scaffold and support interpersonal learning in all its forms, and provide a foundation for the effective integration of people components in a learning environment, as well as for nurturing a community of learners that support one another's learning.

LEARNING THROUGH AND WITH OTHER PEOPLE

Learning interactions among people are quite diverse: One worker may call a peer to get advice. A team member pings a colleague on Twitter to get a quick question answered. There's a lively discussion on the company blog about how to best address a new client need. A global work team organizes a multisite test of the new videoconferencing equipment, experimenting with the various tools to learn how to use them effectively. A team of people set up a conference room so they can work together to figure out the best way to reshape a work process to be more efficient and effective. A supervisor coaches a direct report preparing for an important presentation. In many of these interactions, one person may be identified as the learner, and the other as the developer, at least for a specific point in time. In others, the relationship is best described as co-learners. In order for these interactions to result in learning, a degree of intentionality is needed. What we see here is deliberate action that is meant to develop knowledge or skills, and deliberate pursuit of learning.

> Social learning is based on the premise that our *understanding* of content is socially constructed through conversations about that content and through grounded interactions, especially with others, around problems or actions. The focus is not so much on *what* we are learning but on *how* we are learning.
>
> —John Seely Brown and Richard Adler, "Minds on Fire"

This chapter focuses on developing a broad understanding of social learning, which is described as any learning that is precipitated or supported by some kind of interaction with other people. It is not limited to interactions through social media, and it can be one-on-one learning or learning in a group.

Some relationships are deep and ongoing, while others are fleeting and utilitarian, but all of these interactions result in learning for one, both, or all of the participants. The variety of interactions in which learners and developers can engage is captured in Figure 4-1. On the left side are actions that the developer might take: to instruct, coach, and support learners in a variety of ways. On the right are the actions and behaviors of the learner, who actively engages in course work, responds to coaching, connects with a network of developers, and so on.

FIGURE 4-1. PROCESSES OF LEARNING THROUGH RELATIONSHIPS

Learning Through Relationships

Learning

Formal Learning
Observing
Asking
Listening
Note taking

Practice and Coachability
Practicing
Asking for feedback
Responding to feedback

Vicarious Learning
Drawing out lessons
Interpreting stories

Engagement in Reflection
Reflecting out loud
Discussing

Openness
Sharing concerns and fears
Responding to support

Connections
Accessing network
Accessing resources

Work Activity
Applying learning
Collaborating
Working together
Trial and error

Developing

Formal Learning
Teaching
Demonstrating
Role modeling
Scaffolding
Sharing information

Observation and Coaching
Coaching
Assessing
Critiquing
Providing feedback

Personal Openness
Sharing (views, insider info)
Storytelling (personal stories)

Engagement in Reflection
Asking penetrating questions
Active listening

Personal Support
Supporting
Encouraging
Advising
Counseling

Connections
Brokering opportunities
Introducing to contacts
Providing entre into closed circles
Giving resources

Work Activity
Collaborating
Working together
Trial and error

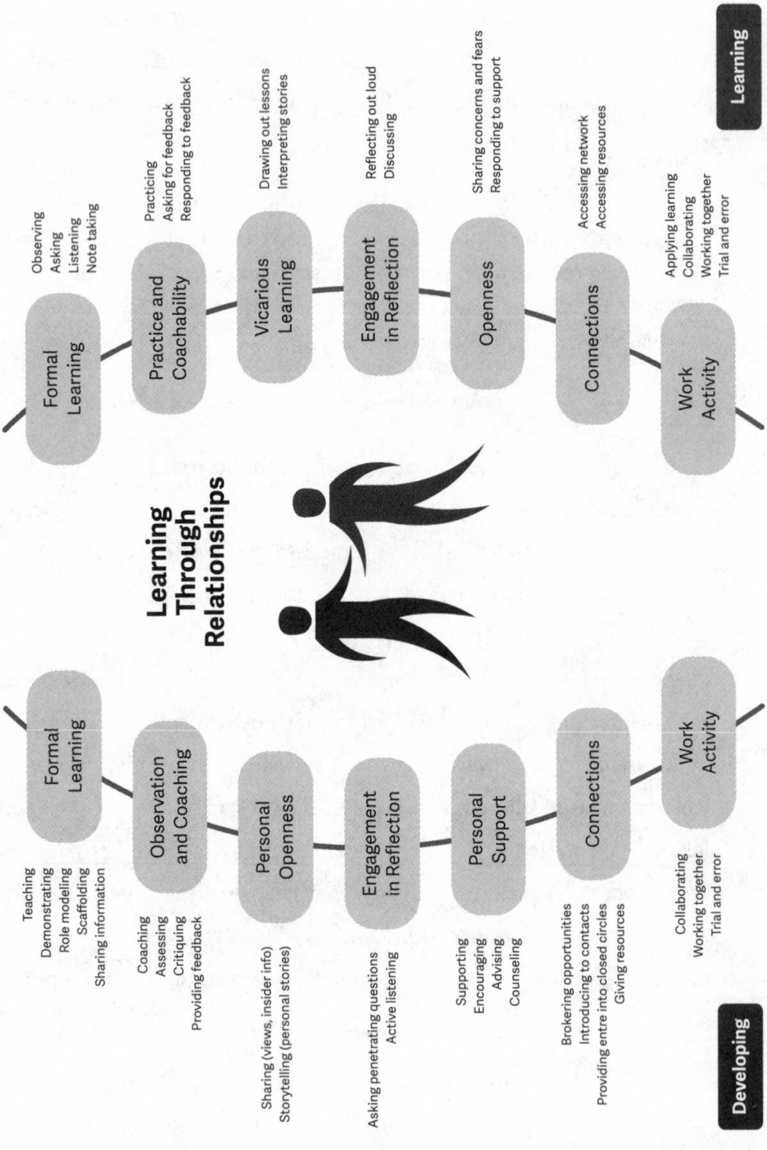

Many of these activities can be conceived as a type of call and response: the trainer teaches and the learner learns; the tenured co-worker acts as a role model, the newbie emulates; the novice practices, the coach critiques; the mentor challenges the learner to think more deeply, the protégé reflects out loud about options and ramifications. It is important to note that in work activity—collaborating, working together, and so on—the dynamics change. Learning *while doing* allows learners and developers to co-create knowledge, fine-tune skills, and define practices. In working together, the distinction between developer and learner often disappears.

Interestingly, studies show that developmental relationships are often mutual—that mentors often learn from protégés, teachers often learn from their students, and new-to-role learners often teach a thing or two to more experienced people as they try to make sense of their new accountabilities.

KEY FACTORS ENABLING SOCIAL LEARNING

Relationships that enable learning and development can have varying levels of depth. Learners can gain knowledge and skills from others without knowing them well on a personal level, as in reading an expert's publications, observing people in action, or engaging in brief exchanges on social media. At the other end of the scale, mentors and protégés and learning-focused work teams engage frequently in many different learning exchanges, often switching between the learner role and the developer role. These deeper relationships require trust and communication.

When you are promoting learning through people in a learning environment, you need to attend to specific factors that support the development of these relationships. Researchers have studied this aspect of learning and have documented three important kinds of factors: individual, relational, and organizational (Rock and Garavan 2006, 2011).

At the individual level (whether a developer or a learner), people need to have the desire to interact, the skills to communicate with one another, and the savvy to network and build relationships. Importantly, they also need to know themselves well enough to identify their learning needs and gifts, and the confidence to learn and experiment with new behaviors. Learner motivation also plays a role here.

At the relational level, there must be a degree of trust and authenticity between a developer and learner. Both parties need to be able to speak candidly with each other, and they have to listen, communicate, and give and receive feedback. Another important aspect that solidifies the relationship is for people to have access to the time, space, and technical tools that allow them to converse. Do not underestimate the importance of time here—it takes time for relationships to strengthen and for trust to build.

At the organizational level, the organization itself needs to support learning and development in various ways, setting an expectation for learning and sharing, and promoting the development of the skills necessary for engaging effectively with one another. In other words, it's helpful to have a strong learning culture in the organization. Relationships can grow without it, but having a learning culture really allows them to flourish.

Based on these findings, you can run through a mental readiness checklist for the learners and developers in your particular situation. You'll find an informal social learning readiness assessment at the end of this chapter (Worksheet 4-1). If you find some factors that are weak, you'll want to identify steps you can take to strengthen them so that developmental relationships can form.

Often the joy and power of learning is inextricable from the amazing people with whom you learn; having colleagues, mentors, coaches, and others who support and catalyze your learning is a treasure. Learning environments are most impactful when the "people" part contributes significantly to learning, and we can design elements into learning environments that promote this kind of interpersonal exchange.

DESIGNING PROGRAMS

One of the ways we enable social learning in a learning environment is crafting formal development programs, such as mentoring programs, peer onboarding, coaching, and peer learning events (such as book studies, discussion groups, action learning groups). Given these factors, there are a number of actions we can take to ensure the success of these programs.

- To solidify individual factors:
  o Help learners and developers become aware of their strengths and weaknesses and identify goals. This can be facilitated through self-assessment and action planning.
  o Provide activities that encourage learners to seek out others for conversation, specific learning, or advice.

- o Promote motivation and self-direction using strategies discussed in chapter 3.

- o If you are developing a program, be sure to define its purpose and consider selecting people based on their willingness and ability to engage in this way.

- o Support the development of the interpersonal and communication skills necessary to engage.

- To solidify relational factors:

  - o Ensure some level of compatibility by looking at goals, areas of expertise, career trajectories, personality types, and other factors. (Attempts at "matching" people have shown mixed success in the research, but may be helpful in your situation.)

  - o Provide guidance for interaction—specific goals, checklists, and discussion topics, for example, especially for mentoring and coaching relationships.

  - o Encourage and enable the pair to meet frequently. Recommend specific timeframes, frequency, and distraction-free locations to meet, and provide quality online conferencing tools where needed. In a hectic work environment, this may be one of the most critical keys to success.

- To solidify organizational factors:

  - o Work with organizational leadership to strengthen the overall learning culture, and identify and remove barriers to learning.

  - o Provide support for learning continuous improvement practices and feedback skills in general if needed.

THE ROLE OF SOCIAL MEDIA

Social media has been a boon to relational learning insomuch as it enables the processes described so far. Through the Internet, people can connect with others that they may never meet face-to-face. They can interact with thought leaders, learn what other organizations are doing, listen in on industry-wide conversations, and find out about new resources, articles, and learning opportunities.

Some of the connections made through social media are "loose ties"—people who can be influential and who can share learning resources, but with whom there is no deep personal connection. At the same time, social media has made it possible to build strong relationships with people whom one may have had little opportunity to meet and engage with otherwise. Just like developing relationships in the physical world, deepening cyber-based connections with "friends" and "followers" requires consistent interaction and more personal disclosure.

Both loose ties and deep relationships can be promoted and nurtured through the use of social media. In creating a learning environment, it can be important to have a variety of social media tools through which people can interact. Some of these tools may be connected outside the organization (such as blogs, Twitter, and social networking sites), while others may need to be limited to connections inside an organization's security firewall.

When social media advocates explain how their networks are valuable for their learning, they cite a substantial list of benefits. At its core, social media helps learners connect with others in their fields who are discussing emerging trends and tackling similar challenges.

These connections often point out relevant resources (such as articles, websites, books, and conferences), and engage in online discussions about emerging ideas and issues. A social network can often be the quickest source of answers to urgent questions. Even without posting to the web, a learner can have access to important ideas and news.

Benefits also accrue from what learners share as much as from what they find through social media; social media learning comes from what you give as well as what you get. The act of writing forces people to clarify their thoughts (at least a bit), transforming a set of impressions and random ideas into a cohesive narrative. By "working out loud" in this way, people increase the likelihood that they'll get useful feedback on their ideas and support for their work. In addition, a timeline of social posts provides a record of notes that can be searched later, and can be a quick way to ensure that ideas are not forgotten. Social media use can also help cement a person's professional reputation.

Here are some questions you can ask when considering the social media strategy for your learning environment:

- What social media tools do learners *already use,* and how can we use those tools to enable learning? (Don't assume that people already know how to use the tools to support their learning.)

- What social media tools are *available* for learners to leverage (outside and inside the enterprise)?

- Who are the people that learners should "follow" or "friend"? What tools are they using?

- What are the best ways to enable and promote asynchronous interactions that support learning?

- Which online conversations can be more public (on the Internet) and which need to be limited to tools inside the enterprise (for reasons of privacy and security)?

- How can we promote the use of social media among learners who have little experience (or inclination) to use it for learning?

- What social media policies are in place, and were they developed with learning in mind?

LEADING A COMMUNITY OF LEARNERS

When you have a group of learners who already have a relationship with one another (a work team, a course cohort, or a group that has similar challenges and a desire to learn from one another), then supporting their ongoing learning with a robust learning environment can be a real boost to their cohesion as a learning community. Through effective learning environment design, you can give them additional learning materials, space for shared documentation, and new communication channels that will be welcome and well utilized.

The most important community-building tool is direct conversation, so it is important to open up channels that allow the community to engage with one another. These channels can be both direct and electronic: meetings, video and audio communication, discussion boards, instant messaging or Twitter, and other means of interacting both synchronously and asynchronously.

It can be important to have a community manager or advisory team for your learning environment who takes on the role of actively promoting interaction and sharing among members of the group. A community manager builds the community by:

- getting to know community members one-on-one, and becoming familiar with their projects and learning needs
- introducing people to one another, especially when they have specific needs or projects in common
- prompting community members to post ideas, questions, and resources to the community space
- ensuring that community members get their questions answered in a timely manner
- inviting contributions and interactions by experts
- sharing stories of what individuals in the community are accomplishing
- deliberately generating conversations among community members by posting provocative or compelling content, asking interesting questions, and bringing together like-minded members who are working on similar challenges
- keeping an ear to the ground for emerging needs of the community and proactively finding and curating resources that may be helpful
- moderating the online experience, managing technical problems, and thwarting any disruptive activity
- garnering support from leaders, key stakeholders, and other needed advocates
- measuring and reporting on community outcomes.

Enabling the learners to cultivate the environment will also help to ensure its success. By actively involving learners in planning and curating the environment, you greatly increase the chances that they will endorse the materials and activities you've assembled. Learners can help flag the best resources and identify those that are unhelpful or have become outdated. Most importantly, members of the community can also be authors of the resources—creating articles, tip sheets, videos, and other learning resources for the community's shared knowledge base.

When a group of people already have relationships with one another, the social aspects of the learning environment can get strong reviews; learners may respond well to having new ways to interact, especially when the environment provides connection to experts. Conversely, it can be more difficult to promote community activity when the learners have only loose ties to one another. In this case, a designer must go well beyond building the infrastructure for community interaction. If you simply collate resources and open up a discussion forum for learners who do not already have a working relationship, you are not likely to find success—at least not in generating discussion among learners. They probably won't know one another, be invested in one another's success, or have the kind of trust (in one another or the organization) that would allow them to interact effectively in a public forum.

Consider, for example, that you have assembled a learning environment to support manager development. Managers may not yet see the potential that exists in everyone relying on one another for learning support and problem resolution. Or you may be assembling an environment for newcomers who have barely met each other. Or your learning environment may be for a geographically dispersed user group who work in varying organizations and industries—they don't know who the go-to people are, and they are not sure whether to trust one another. In these instances, you are assembling an environment to serve the needs of a learner group that doesn't already have deep connections.

Many theorists would caution against trying to create a community where none exists, but some organizations have had success in building a community over time. The role of the community manager is critical in this instance, and all of the activities described in this chapter need to be consistently enacted. The resources listed in the additional resources section provide additional advice for building communities.

WORKSHEET 4-1. SOCIAL LEARNING READINESS ASSESSMENT

This assessment may help you to determine whether your learners are likely to engage with one another.

Rate each item on the following scale.

3 = to a great extent   2 = to some extent   1 = to little extent

Base your ratings on where you think the majority of learners would fall. Estimate ratings where you are unsure. Score "0" if you are not even able to estimate a rating.

Learner Readiness

To what degree do *learners* demonstrate:

___ Knowledge of their own strengths and weaknesses?

___ Confidence or a developmental mindset?

___ Ability to set their own goals?

___ Motivation to learn in this arena?

___ An ability to learn?

___ Strong networking skills?

___ Strong interpersonal skills?

Total: ___ / 21 = ___ %

WORKSHEET 4-1. (CONTINUED)

Developer Readiness

To what degree do *developers* demonstrate:

___ Knowledge of their own strengths and weaknesses?

___ Confidence or a developmental mindset?

___ Ability to set goals?

___ Motivation to develop others in this arena?

___ An ability to facilitate learning in others?

___ Strong networking skills?

___ Strong interpersonal skills?

Total: ___ / 21 = ___ %

Relational Readiness

To what degree does *the pair or group as a whole* demonstrate:

___ Compatibility?

___ Opportunity to get together?

___ An atmosphere of trust that values authenticity?

___ Willingness to engage in deep conversation with one another?

___ Ability to be reflective in that relationship?

___ Ability to give and receive candid developmental feedback within that relationship?

Total: ___ / 18 = ___ %

WORKSHEET 4-1. (CONTINUED)

Organizational Readiness

To what degree does *the organization* exhibit:

___ A culture that values and promotes learning and development?

___ Real encouragement of sharing across the organization?

___ A majority of people skilled at giving and receiving feedback?

___ A structure that supports continuous improvement?

Total: ___ / 12 = ___ %

Use these percentages as a rough estimate of the degree of readiness in each of the areas that influence the formation of developmental relationships. Where the degree of readiness causes concerns, consider taking action to strengthen the weak items. This chapter should provide you with some ideas about what to do.

Note: This survey provides an indicator of developmental relationship readiness drawn from research-based factors, but it is not a validated instrument.

CONCLUDING THOUGHTS

People are critical to learning, and effective learning environment design not only links people to one another, but also encourages the kind of interactions that promote learning and development. For each learning environment design project, you will need to determine the most impactful ways that you can promote and support interaction. In some instances, that work will be quite easy, as you tap into relationships that already exist or are fairly simple to make and strengthen. In other projects, however, you may struggle to figure out how to incorporate more people components into your vision. While solid productive learning relationships can't be forced, the research synthesized in this chapter gives you a foundation on which you can begin to build your strategies for promoting social learning.

5

Learning Environments in Academic Contexts

Faculty and course designers in higher education are also being urged to think beyond the context of a fixed course or curriculum. In many fields, the knowledge base and skill set needed to be effective in practice is advancing at a brisk pace. Faculty recognize that they need to prepare students for continuously developing and updating their skills, even as they are in the process of learning foundations and current practices.

A number of other influences are driving faculty to rethink traditional approaches. Many desire to have a long-term influence on the professional lives of their students. They strive to create what Dee Fink (2013) calls "significant learning experiences" that linger with students and ignite their ongoing desire to immerse themselves in a field or area of practice. Experiences with the MOOC (massive open online course) phenomenon have underscored the value of a learning community—and that is true whether students are in traditional programs or cobbling together formal credits on a quest of their own (see, for example, Funnell 2014). Faculty who have embraced the idea of connected learning, open education, and connectivist MOOCs are continuing to explore ways to build students' 21st-century learning skills—helping them learn how to leverage the value of the web and build their networks in ways that will both support their learning and put them in a position to co-create the knowledge and skills necessary for the future.

For all of these reasons, faculty members are looking for ways to give learners access to reference materials, help them build long-term professional connections, and support the development of web-based lifelong learning skills. Learning environments can be a way to achieve these ends.

ACADEMIC APPLICATIONS FOR LEARNING ENVIRONMENTS

As in the corporate environment, there are a number of ways that learning environments can be conceived. Chapter 1 touched on blended learning hubs, knowledge exchanges, learning portals, and collaboratories. These can be adapted for use in an academic context (see Table 5-1), although they may be better conceptualized at the department level than at the course level to include a wider array of materials and a larger potential learner group.

TABLE 5-1. ACADEMIC INTERPRETATIONS OF LEARNING
ENVIRONMENT STRATEGIES

Strategy	Possible Academic Interpretations
Blended Learning Hub	• Offer students extra materials for exploration and practice. • Guide students to continue their learning beyond the course.
Knowledge Exchange	• Leverage the experience that students bring into their studies of a particular subject. • Have students share their projects and experiences for others to use as learning resources.
Learning Portal	• Contextualize a curriculum and share additional resources for student learning. • Help students understand the connection of each course to an overall strategy for developing a knowledge base or skill.
Collaboratory	• Provide a space where students can work on the leading edge of their fields, applying what they learn to co-creating new approaches, frameworks, or theories.

Learning environment design concepts can also be applied to other emerging strategies in higher education as described in the following sections.

Connected Course

A learning environment might be a way to organize a learner-centered constructivist course. Its purpose would be to give learners access to a wide range of materials and activities on a topic, and to connect learners and experts as a way of creating a rich environment for learner-driven exploration and discussion. Learners themselves define and fine-tune their learning objectives and determine which activities they want to engage. Some MOOC structures achieve the same ends (notably those based on connectivist or constructivist principles).

Connected courses are held online, and often include people who are not taking the course for credit; these may be interested learners and leading thinkers or practitioners in the field at hand.

The faculty and course designers for a connected course start by curating resources in a variety of formats that can be the foundation of an exploration of a given topic or skill. They set up systems that connect learners to one another, and suggest a variety of hands-on activities that challenge learners to share their knowledge and skill for others to comment on and leverage for their own learning. They also invite thought leaders and authors to share their perspectives in open conversations. Gartner Campbell (2014) has described the approach as focusing "joint attention" on a particular topic. The learners and facilitators bring resources and ideas to the table, and then each member of the group uses those that are relatable and helpful.

Grading in such courses (when necessary) is frequently based on materials that the students produce—either through a presentation showing what they've learned, or projects that apply the learning to a particular practice problem.

Workforce Development Site

Some academic programs are developed for the express purpose of preparing students for a specific job or job family. A college or university might launch a workforce development site for a specific initiative to support students in their preparation beyond completing a defined curriculum. The site might be designed to increase interest in the program, enrich the student experience, or encourage ongoing learning and skill development. Connecting students to one another and to potential employers may also be an important aspect of the success of the workforce development effort.

Knowledge Resource Site

The role of a scholar is to deepen our knowledge in a particular arena, and faculty members can sometimes be disappointed in the reach of their work. While one of their goals may be to disseminate knowledge, the work they do is often available only to their own students, readers of academic journals, and fellow researchers. To affect practice, and to continue to enrich the knowledge and practice of students who cross their paths, faculty can also design websites that serve as learning environments for their knowledge base and research.

On a personal site, or a site dedicated to the topic of interest, faculty members can curate a range of resources and activities for peers, students, and other interested individuals. Content-rich webpages, reference lists, articles, curated links, multimedia materials, blog posts, and Twitter feeds can all be collated into a valuable resource. Faculty might also hold old-fashioned "salons," new-fangled "hangouts," or webinars to have more open conversations about their work and interests. Collaborating on such a site with fellow scholars might be a rewarding and impactful endeavor.

Open Wiki

Faculty members can also encourage students to contribute to and continuously update a learning environment about a particular topic or skill. This could be housed on a wiki site or a website maintained by faculty and students on an ongoing basis. Similar to the knowledge website application, a wiki would serve as an ongoing resource—but it would be built by students and constantly updated by successive classes so that it becomes a favorite reference for those interested in the topic.

Student Services Site

In addition to learning environments tied to the content and skills related to various academic disciplines, learning environments may also be useful for academic support services and student development resources. Sites might be imagined for study skills, career planning and job search skills, student leadership development, first-year orientation, "one book" programs, academic advising, and more. These environments may have online and offline components that generate interest, bring people together, and provide resources.

COMPONENTS IN ACADEMIC ENVIRONMENTS

The learning environment design framework describes six categories of components: resources, people, training and education, development practices, experiential learning practices, and learner motivation and self-direction. These component categories are still a useful design framework in the academic context, although they play out a bit differently.

Learner Motivation and Self-Direction

Learner motivation and self-direction underpin the success of a learning environment. Students often come to academic programs more motivated to achieve a credential than to necessarily learn specific knowledge bases and skills developed in particular courses. And, despite the fact that we are several decades into the digital revolution, they are often still anticipating traditional educational approaches in which their learning approach is structured by a teacher. Faculty and course designers who want to use a learning environment approach (or some hybrid thereof) must incorporate materials and activities specifically designed to promote learner motivation. And they should use the approach as a way to scaffold, teaching students how to manage their own learning processes.

People are motivated to learn when they understand how the learning will be applied and they value the potential outcomes. Contextualizing learning is critical, and no more so than when you are working with students who may have little experience on which to base their understanding of application possibilities. It's often very valuable, then, to invite those who do the work to share their experiences and inspire students. Videos, guest speaking engagements, and careful selection of readings may provide this kind of spark for students.

Once students are interested, they may be expecting the professor to tell them what they need to know and give clear directions and criteria for learning. To develop 21st-century learning skills and the ability to continuously learn for a lifetime of rapid change, faculty can devise strategies that scaffold learners through a process that can be engaged later as a self-directed strategy. Suggesting learning paths, giving loose structures, providing examples, and facilitating students' co-creation of outputs and collaboration on quality criteria are just a few of the scaffolding strategies that might be imagined.

Resources

Finding the resources to enrich student learning is probably easy; faculty often leave out many potential reading assignments when they put together course plans. But curating those resources is critical— identifying those that are most readable and relatable, those that spark interest and debate, and those that you would want people to access if they could only access a few. It's also important that you look beyond academic sources to locate additional resources; practitioner-focused journals, recorded webinars, and blog posts can often fire up students and young professionals more than academic material can. Students want multimedia material, so it is a good idea to diversify the kinds of resources you curate for your environment.

Imagine the threads that students may want to follow in exploring a topic and try to give a variety of options for digging deeper. Provide links to other portals that offer resources in your subject area (and closely related areas) to help students see what is available. Annotating and categorizing the resources will also help students find what they are looking for to extend their learning along particular lines.

People

Promoting the growth of professional networks is often a critical piece of the ongoing learning and development picture. You can identify the people learners should follow and provide social media links for experts who have an online presence; these give students a real opportunity to get connected to current conversations in the field. You may also be able to provide a platform through which learners can connect with one another even beyond their years of schooling. Opportunities for working with others on projects and interning with particular experts would provide valuable connections for your students.

Training and Education

It is certainly appropriate to highlight courses that you and your colleagues teach. For extended study, you might recommend a course in another college or university, or free courses structured as MOOCs. You may also be aware of seminars and workshops that are offered by experts in the field. In the case of academic support services and student development, you may include training and education programs as part of the overall effort.

Development Practices

In corporate environments, the development practices category refers to programs and activities that are initiated and led by managers in the company. In an academic context, you might consider listing opportunities you can offer that will help develop students' knowledge and skills. Working on a research project, engaging in book discussions, participating in internships with faculty coaching and supervision, gathering students socially for networking, and the like would fall under this umbrella. Requiring or supporting students in creating an e-portfolio is another way of helping them bridge the space between academic study and practice.

Experiential Learning Practices

Problem-based learning, real-world capstone projects, and other hands-on work can give students real experience that solidifies their learning. Students often report that these are among the most valuable activities they engage in while at college. In addition to offering experiences, though, help students to make meaning of those experiences by reflecting on and processing what they learned and how they can apply that to future endeavors. Be sure to offer the means by which students can begin to evaluate their own success in enacting the practices of their profession. Quality checklists, self-monitoring processes and forms, observation guides, and other supports give learners a way of checking themselves in their attempts to implement what they have learned.

CONCLUDING THOUGHTS

There are many predictions and suggestions about where higher education practices are heading, and it is clear that reinvention may be in order. There is some consensus around wanting graduates to be better prepared for lifelong learning and productivity—to learn effective communication (in the digital age), critical thinking, ethical decision making, research, and self-directed learning skills as much if not more than a body of knowledge and set of specific professional skills. These may be best developed through course structures that provide more application activities than knowledge testing. Rather than having a grade point average as evidence of learning in the college setting, students and employers may instead want to see outcome portfolios and evidence of deep skill development.

In addition to the ways that faculty adopt and fine-tune active teaching practices, a strategy that supports continued learning and the development of a network of experts and colleagues would be welcome. Learning environment design is one such strategy that can be conceived and implemented by individual faculty members (or a small group of colleagues) without waiting for a complete change in the way higher education is packaged and delivered.

6

The Future of Learning

Part of what makes working in learning and development so exciting is the fact that it is an ever-changing field with new technologies, challenges, and opportunities emerging every day in both corporate and higher education contexts. When you couple changes in our approaches to learning with changes in the world at large, you get a dynamic and fascinating playground for our work.

There are a number of workplace and education trends and challenges that will keep learning professionals on their toes in the coming years. This chapter outlines many examples, but the additional resources section also lists several resources you can check out for more in-depth coverage.

Longstanding volatility in the business environment. Business leaders continue to be battered by an ever-changing environment, which is influenced by market fluctuations, global opportunities and pressures, increasingly diverse workforce demographics, expanding and changing technology platforms and tools, and political and regulatory uncertainty. These forces also affect learning strategy. These rapid changes require learning on the fly, and L&D must learn to anticipate competency development needs and respond with curated resources as quickly as possible. Education providers need to be able to be more responsive to these changing needs as well.

Overwhelming speed of change and explosion of available information. It is becoming impossible to keep up with our modern environment. Employees desperately need strategies for filtering information and adopting changes that help them to remain focused on the task at hand. Collaboration is key here as employees can share what they find important and help one another stay current. L&D can support employee efforts by providing tools and dedicated learning advisers. In academic preparation for careers, some knowledge may become outdated even before students graduate, so developing the ability to learn continuously is becoming more critical.

Increasing understanding that modern employee performance depends on the connected and collaborative worker. Employees need strong networks inside and outside their organizations, and they must learn how to effectively collaborate both across the table and across geographical distances. Informal social learning and the ability to use technology to connect to resources and people as needed are becoming essential skills. Organizations are continuing to find ways to connect employees through social learning and performance systems, and they will increasingly issue smartphones and tablets (or create bring-your-own-device policies) to enable immediate electronic access to performance support and communications any place, anytime. Learning resources need to be just as connected, collaborative, and portable.

Increasing interest in and commitment to mobile learning. A further implication of the connected and collaborative worker trend is the recognition that in many situations, learners are just as likely to access learning resources on a smartphone or tablet as on a desktop computer. Companies may even be more interested in creating custom enterprise apps for learning and performance support. Learning resources need to be accessible and usable on smaller devices and in short spans of time. Learning projects that require a greater investment of time can also be supported by mobile follow-up and support materials.

Expanding attention on customized, personalized, and adaptive learning. While these terms have different meanings, they all focus on a more learner-centric view of learning—ways of delivering to learners the exact modules they need in an appropriate timeframe. A learning environment takes that one step further by giving learners control over the resources they select.

Ever-evolving technology. Any look into the future should try to anticipate how newer technologies might support learning and performance. The items that are immediately emerging at this writing include wearable technology, the Internet of things, and 3-D printing. Designers are imagining how to make access to resources even more efficient with wearable computers and specialized devices. The Internet of things movement considers how connecting data flows from separate sources might make decision making easier (or even unnecessary as algorithms process data and respond accordingly). Three-dimensional printing can make physical resources handier, allowing for the creation of unique props for learning. In addition to these emerging areas, advances in mobile learning are a continuing trend, necessitating shorter bytes of learning support on smaller-screen platforms. All of these open up possibilities for new resources and activities for learning that can be incorporated into a learning environment.

Continued commitment to measurement of outcomes. Both employers and employees are interested in ensuring that they demonstrate outcomes from the investment in learning. There may be more interest in "badging" strategies (which document skills and capabilities) than in academic credentialing, which has proven to be an unreliable indicator of knowledge base and skill. A measurement strategy related to learning environments, therefore, might need to include ways for learners who are following their own paths to document their skill building along the way.

Deepening focus on engagement. Employers understand the value of having engaged employees, and they are instituting workplace policies and practices that support engagement. Being able to learn and develop on the job is a big part of what engages employees; so learning strategy is critical to an organization's engagement efforts. It's important that employees are quickly brought up to speed when they begin a job, and that they are well supported in continuing to deepen their knowledge base and skills, both independently and in collaboration with others.

Continued focus on analytics. Big data is here to stay, and the learning and development field is not immune to its influences. Learning leaders must understand analytics and work to define appropriate, proactive, and impactful measures that support decision making and planning—well beyond simply reporting activities and outcomes. Using data to customize learning recommendations is especially important.

Decreasing willingness to invest in employee development. Employers want to hire people who are already skilled for the job, and they don't want to pay for development that makes employees more marketable to other employers. This puts employees in the awkward position of having to manage their own development, without necessarily being granted the financial resources or time to do so. In this environment, L&D organizations need to support employees by providing guidance for self-development, especially the kind of self-development that costs little or nothing in terms of real currency. Promoting learning environments can be a robust yet inexpensive way to advocate for employee development.

Increasing investment in leader development. Employers view leader development as a critical need, and it is the one area in which they are willing to invest time and resources. They hope to ensure the organization's future and entice longer-term leader commitment by ensuring continuous development for up-and-coming leaders. Leader development requires experiential learning and other nonformal strategies of learning on the job. L&D can add tremendous value by understanding and supporting these kinds of learning processes in the leader development context (as well as in other contexts).

These additional trends affect people working in higher education environments:

Shifting value of degree programs and lessening of confidence in colleges and universities to prepare workers for the workplace. It is unclear where we expect employees to gain the skills they need if not through academic programs. New systems of workforce development may come into play, and there are a number of options on the table that bear watching: increasing use of badging, competency-based education that focuses on validating specific acquired skills, certification programs from reputable vendors and academic institutions, apprenticeships with leading practitioners or industry mavericks, and mentoring and coaching strategies. Program designers in college and university settings are under pressure to demonstrate the value of educational goals and outcomes. Education is less about transmitting bodies of knowledge and more about developing lifelong skills, although both are important. This has implications for course design as educators seek to create relevant and challenging learning activities to ensure educational outcomes with long-term impact.

Contextualized learning. To deepen learning and improve retention of knowledge and skills developed in a degree program, higher education instructors are increasingly moving toward contextualized activities. This need requires designing deeply engaging application activities and developing more partnerships between schools and businesses.

Open educational resources. Integration of open Internet-based resources as content for courses continues to grow, especially as resentment deepens for expensive firewalls surrounding published materials, and concern grows over textbook costs for students and subscription services costs for libraries. Like their corporate counterparts, academics are recognizing that the quality of resources openly available on the web makes compiling customized reading materials much easier. A designer's ability to find, filter, and curate materials becomes more valuable.

Open learning and domain of one's own. More higher education instructors are finding value in having students compile their learning assets outside a closed course management system, so they can continue accessing the networks they build and the materials they create even after graduation. Encouraging open and connected learning also prepares students more effectively for lifelong self-directed learning.

IMPLICATIONS

To provide value in this kind of environment, learning professionals need to expand their reach and support learning in all its forms. Developing a deep understanding of social learning, informal learning, peer-to-peer learning practices, performance support, experiential learning, organizational learning cultures, and similar approaches enables learning professionals to devise comprehensive strategies that utilize what is already available in the environment to support ongoing learning.

This approach to supporting learning requires new skills: Internet savvy, curation skills, networking and collaboration capabilities, business acumen, comfort with changing technology, and consulting and influence skills, to name a few. Learning professionals need to manage their own development in exactly the ways all learners must manage it—by finding the right resources, following the leaders, collaborating with peers, and keeping their fingers on the pulse of what's next.

Valued roles in the learning and development space are also shifting. Pundits are predicting that organizations will value learning coaches—people who can help others solidify learning goals, find appropriate resources, and effectively apply learning in the workplace. This is a more customized, one-on-one role than we have seen in the past. Learning professionals need to be effective curators as much as effective designers and facilitators. The ability to build relationships, promote learning in the workflow, and identify quality resources will also be necessary to be successful in the emerging L&D environment.

THE ROLE OF LEARNING ENVIRONMENTS

Learning environments by design—or other approaches that are equally comprehensive and diversified—are becoming the future of learning strategy. A learning advocate's ability to locate relevant resources and guide learners to engage with people and activities that help them develop can be more valuable (and more timely) than his or her ability to design an effective course. Formal programs aren't going away, but they are only the beginning of learning—a way of grounding key concepts and skills that can be infinitely built upon as emerging knowledge and practices come to the fore and the work environment shifts.

This book has provided frameworks and process advice for crafting learning environments. The processes of envisioning, finding, curating, assembling, and cultivating learning environments engage and align with the living, ever-evolving nature of the recommendations you are making. Whether you are creating a blended learning hub, a knowledge exchange, a learning resource portal, a collaboratory, or some combination or new form of environment, the concepts discussed in these pages will help ground your work and create a strong strategy. The learning environment components chart (see Figure 1-1) provides a checklist of potential materials and activities for inclusion in the environment and acts as a reminder of all the ways that learning can be supported in the workplace. The learning environment blueprint helps you conceptualize and communicate your recommendations for supporting learning in dynamic modern workplaces.

CONCLUDING THOUGHTS

Even if we perfect the ability to instantly transfer knowledge and skills through an implanted microchip in our brains, learning will always be as necessary to life as breathing. The digital age provides us with access to documented knowledge, people, emerging practices, new ideas, amazing tools, and so much more, which promises to help us keep up with a world that evolves minute by minute.

Learning leaders can provide real support by helping employees access the best resources and collaborate with one another in learning and revising work practices every day. I hope the learning environment design framework assists you in strategizing learning in our modern world.

The learning environment design strategy is ever-evolving, and additional resources and iterations have been posted to www.L4LP. com. I welcome feedback and suggestions at clombardozzi@L4LP .com.

> Learning is not attained by chance. It must be sought for with ardor and attended to with diligence.
>
> —Abigail Adams

Appendix: Learning Environment Blueprints

In this section, you'll find three examples of learning environment blueprints. These are all globalized fictitious examples based on specific experiences and scenarios.

You can also find examples of learning environments on the Internet as many people and organizations have embraced the value of curating resources for specific purposes. Professional organizations, government entities, vendors, authors, and others often provide learning resources for their constituents. You'll be able to see a reflection of learning environment design concepts and ideas in their structure, and you can note the ways that they are effective and ineffective to give you further input for your own designs.

Sales Team Onboarding Resources

BACKGROUND

This environment plays off the story of Cara and Yuri from the introduction. We imagined an L&D team curating a learning resource portal for the newest members of a sales team so that they could quickly locate the information they need to come up to speed and gain foundational skills. The salespeople are expected to know what they need to know to some degree.

There might well be opportunity to expand this learning environment to bring in resources and activities that will help the more experienced and tenured salespeople to fine-tune their skills, but in this scenario, the focus is exclusively on onboarding.

PURPOSE

Guide salespeople to the most useful resources for self-directed learning.

CONTEXT

Business goals supported:

- Increase sales by 20 percent over the next two years.

Relevant performance objectives:

- Establish adviser relationships with decision makers in territory.

- Maintain book of business year after year.

- Oversee preparation of request for proposal (RFP) responses for potential clients in territory.

RELEVANT LEARNER CHARACTERISTICS

- New hire salespeople

- May have some sales experience or some internal company experience

- Expected rate of hiring is four to ten per year
- Geographically dispersed around the United States

TOPIC AND SCOPE

- Focus on first six to twelve months on the job—help new hires come up to speed.
- Include both core sales skills and technical information about products and competitors.
- Focus on providing general sales skills found to be successful in this environment, rather than materials to deepen all competencies necessary for long-term success.

INITIAL COMPONENTS

NOTE: All materials on this component list are fabricated for illustration purposes.

RESOURCES

Orientation:

- Home office in a box (how-tos for systems and technology)
- Transition playbook (information on clients in territory)
- Corporate onboarding resource site
- Sales incentive information pages

Product and industry information:

- Competitor intelligence materials (website links, analysis, whitepapers)
- Sales portal (detail product information, product briefing sheets, marketing materials, archived sales team webinars)
- Product app for smartphones
- RFP database (copies of all RFPs tagged with categories for easy search)

- Sales bulletin and archive (monthly newsletter that includes news, tips, profiles, upcoming events, and more)
- Industry news feeds

Sales skills resources:

- Books provided electronically or in paper form
- Success stories (internally recorded interviews that break down lessons learned from big wins)
- Trusted adviser webinar series (recorded)
- Sales superstar podcast subscription (vendor materials; many topics available and downloadable)
- Access to The Sales Professional article database
- Suggested Twitter feeds (provide at least six)

PEOPLE

- Assigned mentor for onboarding period
- Team member profiles on company website (make it searchable and include skills profile and client experience)
- Sales team asynchronous discussion board and messaging tools
- Quarterly regional informal get-togethers
- Sales Institute membership (or similar professional organization)

TRAINING AND EDUCATION

- Sales simulation e-learning
- E-learning series on company products
- Consultative Selling course (or other publicly offered training course)
- Corporate onboarding series

- Annual sales conference (includes concurrent workshops on timely topics)
- Monthly sales team webinars (topical education, usually about new products or competitor information)

DEVELOPMENT PRACTICES

- Coaching guide provided to assigned mentor
- Sales presentation coaching by management team
- Sales call partnering (ride-along)
- Road Ready Assessment (sales manager checklist and assessment to validate new salespeople are up to speed)
- All hands huddle conference calls (arranged by salespeople for assistance with time-sensitive challenges)

EXPERIENTIAL LEARNING PRACTICES

- Observations by experienced sales execs
- Individualized coaching

CULTIVATION PLAN OUTLINE

- The site will be pilot-tested with salespeople who have been hired in the last 12 months.
- The L&D team will be notified when new salespeople are hired, and they will remind managers and mentors of this resource for onboarding new people.
- New hires will be made aware of the resource on their first day on the job (included in a welcome note from the L&D team).
- During the first year, the L&D team will follow up with new hires, their mentors, and their managers once a month over the first three months and again at the end of six months to assess the usefulness of the environment and learn what needs

to be pruned or added. The team will use a quick survey for the evaluation. This practice could be continued beyond the first year, but it will be decided at that time.

- Because the industry is so volatile, the site will be reviewed on a quarterly basis to make sure that the most recent material is available.

- The sales management team will name a senior salesperson as the ongoing "owner" of this project, and that person will be involved in the survey and review process.

NOTES

As you imagine how to assemble this site, it might become apparent that materials will need to be annotated and contextualized so that new salespeople have the background they need to make sense of what they find; otherwise, they may not understand how some of the resources could be utilized.

While the components of this environment were strategized using the component categories, the environment probably won't be organized that way on the company's Internet site. The team will work with web designers to organize the resources so that they can be accessed from several angles, including timeline (week 1, week 2), actions (researching competitors, preparing a sales presentation), and type of resource (books, articles, videos).

Faculty Development Resources for New Adjunct Faculty Members

BACKGROUND

The instructional design (ID) team at Stone College wants to provide more support for new adjunct faculty to become successful in their teaching role. The ID team has already developed several onboarding workshops (webinars), which are blended designs with preview and follow-up resource materials, and one-on-one support and coaching. These have proven to be well received by the faculty, but they have limited scope. The faculty's additional learning needs are more specific and need to be addressed in a timely way, often by calling the ID team for advice and coaching. The ID team has a number of resources they share in these one-on-one conversations.

The ID team hopes that by expanding available online resources, faculty may be able to find what they need in a more timely and efficient way. They envision creating a blended learning hub to expand learning beyond orientation and basic courses. The learning environment will be set up in the college's course management system, and all new adjunct faculty will be automatically enrolled in the "course."

PURPOSE

Provide on-demand resources to support excellence in teaching.

CONTEXT

Relevant faculty tasks and job roles:

- Design and deliver courses to meet the learning objectives as defined by the curriculum plan.
- Engage students actively in learning.
- Effectively integrate technology in teaching.

College goals supported:

- Improve student success rates.
- Improve new faculty student evaluations.
- Reduce new faculty turnover (stay less than two years).

RELEVANT LEARNER CHARACTERISTICS

- Primary focus: new adjunct faculty
- Assume they have expertise in their subject matter, but possibly little background in teaching or course design
- Employed on one campus, but 50 percent of the faculty teach online only and may do so from a distance
- Total number of adjunct faculty: 750; there are 50 to 100 new faculty members every year
- Hired primarily for subject matter expertise

TOPIC AND SCOPE

- Four main topics: course design, online techniques, classroom techniques, and instructional technology.
- Focus on start-up curation and plan for resources to build over time.
- Reorganize and package what is already available and identify high priority additions to find or create.
- Focus on new faculty. Expanding for experienced faculty will be taken up in additional phases of the project.

INITIAL COMPONENTS

GENERAL INFORMATION

- Welcome video
- Faculty mentoring program

- Learning path recommendations (courses and readings based on background and skill)
- Adjunct faculty handbook link

FACULTY DEVELOPMENT COURSES

- Adjunct Faculty Welcome and Orientation
- Core Instructional Design Concepts and Processes
- Creating Engaging Courses
- Online Course Design
- How Students Learn
- Teaching With Technology

COURSE DESIGN

- Design overview (e-learning)
- Syllabus templates
- Required syllabus elements
- A guide to learning objectives
- Syllabus feedback process and request form
- Copyright legalities
- How to arrange an instructional design consultation

GENERAL TEACHING RESOURCES

- My best day (video and essay series about teaching successes by college faculty)
- It worked for me (a database or discussion forum of in-course exercises and techniques, categorized by department and delivery method: classroom, online, or webinar)
- Faculty to faculty (Q&A discussion forum)

- Link to the Faculty Focus newsletter or blog (an external resource)
- Our favorite bloggers (faculty blog roll organized by discipline)
- SlideShare archive (from previous one-off workshops by instructional designers)

CLASSROOM TECHNIQUES

- Recommended resource books (annotated list)
- Links to a selection of articles on effective classroom learning techniques

ONLINE TECHNIQUES

- Recommended resource books (annotated list)
- Links to a selection of articles on effective online learning techniques

TECHNOLOGY RESOURCES

- Course management system (CMS) help links
- CMS tutorial link
- CMS job aids
- Webinar software help link
- Guide to Google Docs
- Projection equipment job aid
- Clickers (Instructions on how to use them effectively and how to reserve for class)

CULTIVATION PLAN OUTLINE

- Most handouts from courses will be linked in the learning environment instead.
- New faculty will be given access automatically, and the ID team leader will send a warm welcome note to introduce resources and services.

- All newly created job aids will be added to the learning environment.

- ID team members will take turns weekly to actively monitor discussions (and comment).

- The ID team will identify popular links and articles shared by faculty in discussion boards and store them in a more permanent part of the environment so they can be retrieved more easily in the future.

- A blog will be instituted to share emerging technologies and ideas for engaging students; guest blogging (authored by faculty) will be encouraged.

- The ID team will review the entire site every July to prune and identify additional resources to add.

- Questions about the learning environment will be added to the ID team satisfaction survey, which is already sent to new faculty at the end of their first term.

NOTES

In this example, you see the way that a set of resources can be curated to form a learning environment that is bound to get richer over time. This team started by drafting an environment based on the specific aspects of a role and pulling together a short list of quality materials and activities. They can add to that over time through a solid cultivation plan.

Notice that the components here are organized topically, rather than by component categories. This approach will make more sense to the stakeholders of this project. However, the resources and activities listed here represent all six categories.

Carving Collaboratory

A suburban amateur carver enjoys learning from fellow enthusiasts, and he was surprised to learn that there were a number of like-minded hobbyists in his town. While he is able to learn from a number of online sources, he much prefers studying craftsmanship person to person. He has gradually gotten to know a few folks well enough to organize a regular meeting for sharing projects, getting tips, and receiving helpful critique on individual techniques.

Over time, the group has started referring one another to web resources and sharing video tips that provide refreshers on lessons they have given one another. It has become clear that a shared website might be a better way to communicate rather than through email. A member's daughter has agreed to set up an online space that will serve their needs. While they might never document it this way, this is a good representation of what the group's collaboratory looks like.

PURPOSE

To support one another in learning and fine-tuning a variety of carving techniques.

CONTEXT

Desired performance:

- To make high-quality carved wooden pieces, such as figurines, home décor items, signs, sculptures, or other handmade treasures.

RELEVANT LEARNER CHARACTERISTICS

- Members are an invited group of men and women in the vicinity of one town; the group currently has 27 members.

- All have access to computers, with varying degrees of comfort in using advanced features.

- All have been carving for a number of years as a hobby, and their styles vary, as well as the kinds of items they create.

- Twelve of the members are retired; the rest have other full-time jobs.

TOPIC AND SCOPE

- Components will focus on carving techniques and tools.

- The primary space for learning from and with one another is the monthly meeting, which is scheduled for the third Saturday of the month from 9 a.m. to 1 p.m.

COMPONENTS

MONTHLY MEETINGS

- Show and tell (and critique)

- Occasional invited speakers and workshops

- Time to carve together and discuss ideas and techniques

ON THE WEBSITE

- Profiles and contact information for members, as well as links to any personal websites and social media sites they want to share.

- Web links organized into the following categories:

    o Favorite websites dedicated to carving

    o Carving supply vendors

    o Regional and national carving shows

    o Online video channels

- An extensive multiple-author blog that is set up to allow members to tag posts with categories, which organize the posts on separate pages or sections on the site. The tags include:
  - o Tool reviews
  - o Carving technique videos
  - o Finishing technique videos
  - o Question and answer forum (Q&A and miscellaneous posts)
  - o Photos (for completed projects and commentary)
  - o Vendor reviews
  - o Upcoming shows
  - o Upcoming workshops and demonstrations

CULTIVATION PLAN OUTLINE

- Member's daughter is on call to play webmaster to tweak the site if the members see additional needs.

- Members will encourage one another to share resources between meetings, and plan to continue some discussions from meeting to online and vice versa.

- Time-sensitive material is scheduled for archiving when posted.

NOTES

This is an example of a learning environment that the learners designed for themselves with help from someone who could assemble the resources effectively. You can imagine the daughter sitting in on a meeting and gathering some ideas about what the group needs, and then attending the next meeting to showcase and tweak the format she put together.

The components can be aligned to categories in the learning environment design framework. There are plenty of resources, and the group adds to them frequently. The meetings and online profiles help connect the learners to one another. Occasional workshops provide training, as do some of the videos. The group has some development and experiential learning practices covered by their commitment to supporting one another through active engagement with the club.

References

Bersin, J., and D. Mallon. 2009. *The Enterprise Learning Framework: A Modern Approach to Corporate Training.* Oakland, CA: Bersin by Deloitte.

Brown, J.S., and R.P. Adler. 2008. "Minds on Fire: Open Education, the Long Tail, and Learning 2.0." *EDUCAUSE Review* 43(1): 16-32.

Burke, L., and H. Hutchins. 2007. "Training Transfer: An Integrative Literature Review." *Human Resource Development Review* 6(3): 263.

Campbell, G. 2014. "Why I Teach." Gardner Writes (blog), September 24. www.gardnercampbell.net/blog1/?p=2394.

Corporate Executive Board (CEB). 2014. *Building a Productive Culture: More Learning Through Less Learning. CEB Learning and Development Leadership Council.* www.cebglobal.com/learning-culture.

Fink, L.D. 2013. *Creating Significant Learning Experiences,* 2nd ed. San Francisco: Jossey-Bass.

Funnell, A. 2014. "Massive Open Online Courses: Does the Rhetoric Match the Reality?" Future Tense (blog), July 16. www.abc.net.au

/radionational/programs/futuretense/a-moocs-education-rhetoric
-and-reality/5598962.

Gottfredson, C., and B. Mosher. 2011. *Innovative Performance Support: Strategies and Practices for Learning in the Workflow.* New York: McGraw Hill.

Hagel, J. III, J. S. Brown, and L. Davison. 2010. *The Power of Pull.* New York: Basic Books.

Hart, J. 2010. "5 Stages of Workplace Learning." Learning in the Social Workplace (blog), May 7. www.c4lpt.co.uk/blog/2010/05/07/5-stages-of-workplace-learning-2.

Hodges, T.K. 2001. *Linking Learning and Performance: A Practical Guide to Measuring Learning and On-the-Job Application.* Boston, MA: Butterworth Heinemann.

Kapp, K.M. 2012. *The Gamification of Learning and Instruction.* Alexandria, VA: ASTD Press; San Francisco: John Wiley & Sons.

Lombardozzi, C. 2013. *With a Little Help From Our Friends: How to Leverage Relationships for Employee and Management Development.* Whitepaper. Learning 4 Learning Professionals. http://l4lp.com/wp-content/uploads/2014/03/Lombardozzi-Help-from-friends-9-24-13.pdf.

Malamed, C. 2015. *Visual Design Solutions: Principles and Creative Inspiration for Learning Professionals.* Alexandria, VA: ATD Press; San Francisco: John Wiley & Sons.

Peters, D. 2014. *Interface Design for Learning: Design Strategies for Learning Experiences.* San Francisco: New Riders.

Rheingold, H. 2012. "Crap Detection 101: How to Find What You Need to Know, and How to Decide If It's True." Chap. 2 in *Net Smart: How to Thrive Online,* by H. Rheingold. Cambridge, MA: MIT Press.

Rock, A.D., and T.N. Garavan. 2006. "Reconceptualizing Developmental Relationships," *Human Resource Management Review* 5(3): 330.

Rock, A.D., and T.N. Garavan. 2011. "Understanding the Relational Characteristics of Effective Mentoring and Developmental Relationships at Work." Chap. 7 in *Supporting Workplace Learning,* edited by Rob F. Poell and Marianne van Woerkom. New York: Springer.

Rosenberg, M.J., and S. Foreman. 2014. *Learning and Performance Ecosystems: Strategy, Technology, Impact and Challenges.* Whitepaper. Santa Rosa, CA: The eLearning Guild.

Thomas, D., and J.S. Brown. 2011. *A New Culture of Learning: Cultivating the Imagination for a World of Constant Change.* Self-published.

Wlodkowski, R.J. 2008. *Enhancing Adult Motivation to Learn,* 3rd ed. San Francisco: John Wiley & Sons.

Additional Resources

INTRODUCTION

Emerging Roles in L&D
Jane Hart, "Emerging New Roles for Learning and Performance Professionals," Learning in the Social Workplace (blog), November 19, 2012. www.c4lpt.co.uk/blog/2012/11/19/new-and-emerging -roles-for-learning-and-performance-professionals.

CHAPTER 1

Personal Learning Environments
"7 Things You Should Know About Personal Learning Environments," Educause, May 12, 2009. www.educause.edu /library/resources/7-things-you-should-know-about-personal -learning-environments.
Harold Jarche, "PKM—Personal Knowledge Mastery," www.jarche .com/pkm.

Communities of Practice

Étienne Wenger-Trayner, "Quick CoP Start-Up Guide," http://
wenger-trayner.com/quick-cop-start-up-guide.

Étienne Wenger-Trayner and Beverly Wenger-Trayner, "Introduction
to Communities of Practice," April 15, 2015. http://wenger-
trayner.com/introduction-to-communities-of-practice.

Nancy White and Darren Sidnick, "Communities of Practice Series
With Darren Sidnick," Full Circle Associates, September 7, 2008.
www.fullcirc.com/2008/09/07/communities-of-practice-series
-with-darren-sidnick-1. (This post contains links to all 10 parts of
this blog series.)

The factors of a performance environment were synthesized from:

Darlene Van Tiem, James Moseley, and Joan Conway Dessinger,
*Fundamentals of Performance Technology: A Guide to Improving People,
Process, and Performance* (Silver Spring, MD: International Society
for Performance Improvement, 2004).

Geary A. Rummler and Alan P. Brache, *Improving Performance: How to
Manage the White Space on the Organizational Chart* (San Francisco:
Jossey-Bass, 1995).

Thomas G. Cummings and Christopher G. Worley, *Organization
Development and Change,* 8th ed. (Mason, OH: Thomson South-
Western, 2005).

CHAPTER 2

Needs Assessment

Deborah Tobey, *Needs Assessment Basics* (Alexandria, VA: ASTD
Press, 2005).

Ryan Watkins, Maurya West Meiers, and Yusra Laila Visser, *A Guide
to Assessing Needs: Essential Tools for Collecting Information, Making
Decisions, and Achieving Development Results* (Washington, DC: The
World Bank, 2012).

Performance Consulting

Darlene Van Tiem, James Moseley, and Joan Conway Dessinger, *Fundamentals of Performance Improvement: A Guide to Improving People, Process, and Performance,* 3rd ed. (Silver Spring, MD: International Society for Performance Improvement, 2012).

Geary A. Rummler and Alan P. Brache, *Improving Performance: How to Manage the White Space on the Organizational Chart* (San Francisco: Jossey-Bass, 1995).

Judith Hale, *Performance Consultant's Fieldbook: Tools and Techniques for Improving Organizations and People* (San Francisco: Pfeiffer, 1998).

The Curation Role in L&D

Curata, *5 Simple Steps to Becoming a Content Curation Rockstar.* www .curata.com/resources/ebooks/5-simple-steps-to-becoming-a -content-curation-rockstar.

David Kelly, "Curation: Beyond the Buzzword—Resources Shared at #ASTDTK13," David Kelly (blog), January 27, 2013. http:// davidkelly.me/2013/01/curation-beyond-the-buzzword-resources -shared-at-astdtk13.

Steven Rosenbaum, *Curation Nation: Why the Future of Content Is Context* (New York: McGraw Hill, 2011).

CHAPTER 3

Primary Underlying Theories for the Pillars of Self-Directed Learning

Gary J. Confessore and Sharon J. Confessore, eds., *Guideposts to Self-Directed Learning: Expert Commentary on Essential Concepts* (King of Prussia, PA: Organization Design and Development, Inc., 1992).

Malcolm Knowles, *The Adult Learner: A Neglected Species* (Houston: Gulf Publishing Company, 1973).

Richard Boyatzis, "An Overview of Intentional Change from a Complexity Perspective," *Journal of Management Development* 25(7): 607-23.

Victoria J. Marsick, Karen E. Watkins, and Barbara Lovin, "Revisiting Informal and Incidental Learning as a Vehicle for Professional Learning and Development," chap. 4 in *Elaborating Professionalism: Studies in Practice and Theory*, edited by Clive Kanes (New York: Springer, 2010).

Classic Work Motivation Theories
David McClelland's Need for Achievement Theory
Edgar Schein's Career Anchor Theory
Victor Vroom's Expectancy Theory.

New Roles as Learning Coaches and One-on-One Advisers
Jane Hart, "Emerging New Roles for Learning and Performance Professionals," Learning in the Social Workplace (blog), November 19, 2012, www.c4lpt.co.uk/blog/2012/11/19/new-and-emerging -roles-for-learning-and-performance-professionals.

Randy Emelo, "Facilitating Social Learning," trainingjournal.com, October 2014, www.riversoftware.com/resources/Facilitating _Social_Learning_TJ_Oct14.pdf.

CHAPTER 4

Developing Communities
Étienne Wenger, Richard McDermott, and William M. Snyder, *Cultivating Communities of Practice: A Guide to Managing Knowledge* (Boston, MA: Harvard Business School Publishing, 2002).

Richard Millington, *Buzzing Communities: How to Build Bigger, Better, and More Active Online Communities* (Fever Bee, 2012).

The Community Roundtable: www.communityroundtable.com.

CHAPTER 5

Connected Learning
Connected Courses MOOC materials: http://connectedcourses.net.

CHAPTER 6

Further Trends in Learning Environment Design
Corporate Executive Board (CEB). *Breakthrough Performance in the New Work Environment: Identifying and Enabling the New High Performer* (Executive Guidance for 2013). www.executiveboard.com/exbd -resources/pdf/executive-guidance/eg2013-annual-final.pdf.

Elaine Beich, "Our Profession: Where We've Been and Where We're Going," ASTD Webcast, March 14, 2014. www.td.org/Digital -Resources/Webcasts/TD/2014/03/Our-Profession-Where-Weve -Been-Where-Were-Going

Josh Bersin, *Predictions for 2014* (Bersin by Deloite, December 2013). http://marketing.bersin.com/predictions-for-2014.html.

L. Johnson, S. Adams Becker, V. Estrada, and A. Freeman. 2014. *NMC Horizon Report: 2014 Higher Education Edition.* Austin: The New Media Consortium. www.nmc.org/publication/nmc-horizon -report-2014-higher-education-edition.

Badging
"Badges," Mozilla Open Badges Project, https://wiki.mozilla .org/Badges.

Acknowledgments

My deepest thanks to all my colleagues, students, and clients whose projects, ideas, feedback, and questions have helped me fine-tune the learning environment design framework and hone my descriptions of it.

In many ways, this is a collaborative effort that draws from ideas shared by other professionals who have a similar interest in sorting out how to best support learning in this digital age. You'll see their names in the references and additional resources section of this book.

To my family and friends who have provided ongoing, genuine support and encouragement, this simple thank you is not near enough, but it is heartfelt.

About the Author

Catherine Lombardozzi is a career work-place learning professional with more than 30 years' experience in the field. As founder of Learning 4 Learning Professionals, she is dedicated to supporting the professional development of designers, facilitators, faculty members, learning consultants, and learning leaders in corporate and academic contexts. Catherine's work emphasizes embracing engaging techniques and leveraging emerging technologies, along with drawing on the insight found in the theory and research base of the field. She contributes to professional conferences and journals, and she teaches graduate-level courses in adult learning, instructional design, learning technology, e-collaboration, and consulting. Catherine holds a doctoral degree in human and organizational learning from George Washington University. You can learn more about her ongoing work and background at www.L4LP.com.

Index

Italicized page numbers indicate figures and tables.

improving environment over time,
63–64

keeping environment fresh, 64–65

nurturing community, 64

curating, of learning environment,
15–16, *16*, *17*, 27, *27*, 48–49, 72

in academic environment, 114,
115, 118

categorizing and tagging, 53–54

contextualizing and highlighting,
54–55

environment pruning and refresh-
ment and, 64–65

filtering, 49–52

making connections and generating
discussion, 55

for self-directed learning, 89

custom context, in learning
environment design process, 54

D

Davison, Lang, 75–76

developer readiness, in social
learning, *107*

development practices

in academic environment, 119

as components of learning
environments, *4*, *7*

in learning design framework, *20*

in learning environment design
process, 34, 51

in sales team onboarding resources
blueprint, 137

developmental relationships.
See social learning

discussion, generating in
curating process, 55

discussions boards, quality
check of, 51

E

ecosystems, for learning, 21–22

Emelo, Randy, 91

emotional engagement,
self-directed learning and, 82

employee development, future
focus on, 127

engagement, in self-directed
learning, *79*, 82–83

assessing strength of, *86*

design tools for, 89

future focus on, 126

tactics for strengthening, *87*

"environment conducive to
learning," 23–24. *See also* learning
environment

envisioning, in learning
environment design process,
27, 27, 30–42

crafting blueprint, 42

defining purpose and performance
context, 34–39, *36*

determining needs, 31–34

getting to know learners, 39–40

solidifying topic and scope, 40–42

e-portfolios, 119